Hot Spots

Also by Dave DeWitt

The Fiery Cuisines (with Nancy Gerlach)
Fiery Appetizers (with Nancy Gerlach)
Texas Monthly Guide to New Mexico
Just North of the Border (with Nancy Gerlach)
The Whole Chile Pepper Book (with Nancy Gerlach)

How to Order:

Quantity discounts are available from the publisher, Prima Publishing, P.O. Box 1260DD, Rocklin, CA 95677; telephone (916) 786-0426. On your letterhead include information concerning the intended use of the books and the number of books you wish to purchase.

U.S. Bookstores and Libraries: Please submit all orders to St. Martin's Press, 175 Fifth Avenue, New York, NY 10010; telephone (212) 674-5151.

Hot Spots

Spicy Recipes from America's Most Celebrated Fiery-Foods Restaurants

Dave DeWitt

Prima Publishing
P.O. Box 1260DD
Rocklin, CA 95677
(916) 786-0426

Typography by Alphatype
Production by Carol Dondrea, Bookman Productions
Copyediting by Amy Pattullo
Interior design by Renee Deprey
Cover design by The Dunlavey Studio
Illustrations by Elizabeth Morales-Denney

Portions of this book originally appeared in *Chile Pepper* magazine. Used by permission.

Library of Congress Cataloging-in-Publication Data

DeWitt, Dave.
   Hot spots : spicy recipes from America's most celebrated fiery-foods restaurants / Dave DeWitt.
     p.   cm.
   Includes index.
   ISBN 1-55958-133-6
   1. Cookery. 2. Spices. I. Title.
TX715.D4953 1991   91-22608
641.6′384—dc20   CIP

92 93 94 95 RRD 10 9 8 7 6 5 4 3 2 1
Printed in the United States of America

For my mother, Barbara,
who taught me how to cook
when I was eight years old.

~~~~~~~~~~

ACKNOWLEDGMENTS

Thanks to the following people who had faith in this project and helped to make it a reality: Robert Spiegel, Mary Jane Wilan, Jennifer Bayse, and the great chefs of America's fiery food restaurants.

CONTENTS

INTRODUCTION

Finally breaking free from their regional roots in Louisiana and the Southwest, chile peppers have now spread all over the country. From Boston to Honolulu, from Seattle to Key West, America's restaurants are serving up innovative gourmet meals based on the fiery heat and the spectacular flavors of the many varieties of chiles.

The concept for a collection of recipes from these restaurants arose from the interest restaurateurs showed in the *Chile Pepper* magazine (which I helped to found in 1987), from its beginning. Many owners and chefs subscribed, wrote letters, and even sent us unsolicited recipes. In response, the magazine began to publish articles about fiery food restaurants, including "Chile Chefs from Coast to Coast," which appeared in our May-June 1990 issue. Soon after, we began to run a regular feature called "Hot Spot," which profiled a restaurant and its chef and owner and included one of their recipes containing chiles.

In the process of editing and testing these recipes, it soon became apparent that the major creators of fiery cuisines these days were talented restaurant chefs. As we learned of various Hot Spots that served creative fiery food, we sent them questionnaires and requested hot and spicy recipes popular with their clientele.

This book represents the wealth of responses received from the restaurants surveyed. Owners and chefs from restaurants in over half the states in the country replied and sent recipes. The restaurants serving fiery food and deserving of a space here varied from elaborate mansions and elegant hotels to casual neighborhood bars. Several caterers are included as well. The chefs and owners are of all stripes; many have led previous lives as school teachers, anthropologists, farmers, and nurses; but all share a love of chile peppers.

The recipes reflect the heritage of many cuisines, ranging from Mexican to Cajun to Asian to East Indian to Caribbean and more. Many of the recipes are highly creative amalgams of several cuisines, so readers should be forewarned that this book was intended not only to present authentic dishes, but also to showcase recipes on the cutting edge of cookery. It is interesting to note that by far the greatest number of recipes submitted contained seafood, which reflects the trend of increasing sea-food consumption in this country.

Since each chef has his or her own personal shorthand for designing and writing recipes, it was quite a challenge to translate them into recipes for use by home cooks. All of the recipes had to fit a standard format for this book, which necessitated many changes in style, syntax, and measurements. In some cases, ingredient amounts were radically adjusted because home cooks certainly would not want to cook in restaurant proportions. For example, one chef sent a recipe which began, "Yield: 250 to 300 empanadas."

Occasionally, we have added ingredients that the chefs assumed cooks would use, but neglected to list, such as butter or cooking oil for sautéing onions. Inconsistencies, like ingredients listed but not appearing in the instructions, were fixed. On one or two occasions, we have provided basic recipes that the chefs called for but did not include, such as a Creole sauce. Except for such minor changes, however, the recipes accurately reflect each chef's creations.

Readers should remember that some chefs change their menus daily, so it is quite possible to visit a given restaurant and discover that a dish in this book is not on the menu. Also, turnover is very high in the business and the owners and chefs of some of these restaurants have undoubtedly changed over the span of a year and a half while this book was in production. For readers wishing to visit these Hot Spots, their addresses are listed in the Appendix.

A brief word on the heat scale used in this book is in order. The pungency of any dish is the result of three factors: the relative heat of each variety of chile pepper used, the degree of dilution with other ingredients, and the mixture with components that tend to cut the heat, such as dairy products. All of these factors have been taken into consideration for the following heat levels used in the recipes.

Mild: Has a discernible tingle.

Medium: Produces some warmth but does not burn significantly.

Hot: Has a pleasurable pungency that burns, lingers, and melds with the complex flavors of a meal.

Extremely Hot: Here the burn nearly overwhelms taste, but it can be tamed by reducing the amount of chile recommended.

Home cooks should remember that some people have accustomed themselves to very hot dishes and some have not. Since it is senseless to serve food that is too hot to be eaten comfortably, cooks should always ask guests about their heat level tolerance and then taste-test the dishes before serving them. We have boldfaced the hot and spicy ingredients in each recipe, so that cooks will readily see what pungent products they are using and can make any adjustments they want to the heat level.

Nearly every recipe here contains chile peppers, so many cooks may not want to compose entire meals from this book but rather to incorporate favored dishes into their standard fare. However, it should be pointed out that a certain subculture of adventurous gourmands (affectionately known as chileheads) now finds it fashionable to construct six-course, all-chile banquets! Whichever way you choose to serve these delicious creations, enjoy!

Chile Peppers
and Sources

A Heated Love Affair
with No Divorce in Sight

Even as late as 1975, who could have predicted that Americans, with their bland meat-and-potatoes diet, would embrace hot and spicy foods with such a fervor? Only one person publicly made such a prediction in face of all the evidence in place. His name was John Phillips Cranwell, the author of the first collection of hot and spicy recipes, *The Hellfire Cookbook* (Quadrangle, 1975). Since then, more than twenty other books have been published, and this one joins them.

In his book, Cranwell coined the phrase "fiery foods," collected recipes from all over the world, and made the following observation: "Fiery food, like alcohol, is habit-forming; once you have acquired a taste for fiery foods you will never again be satisfied with bland fare." That phenomenon is precisely what happened to Americans, and here's how it occurred.

About the time Cranwell published *The Hellfire Cookbook,* Americans were traveling more, visiting exotic locales, and trying new and different cuisines. They were also buying up new cookbooks at a record pace, and the recipes in books like Cranwell's inspired home cooks to experiment with dishes from far-flung places such as Latin America, North Africa, India, and Asia.

Other factors were at work as well. The patterns of immigration shifted dramatically from Europe to Third World countries, and soon ethnic neighborhoods were composed of Vietnamese, Mexicans, West Indians, and many others. Interestingly enough, chile peppers played a dominant role in the cuisines of most of these new immigrants. When they moved to the United States, they transferred their own ingredients and techniques and opened markets and restaurants to duplicate the cuisines of their homeland. Americans, eager now to experience new taste sensations, began dining at these restaurants and enjoying the exotic, highly spiced foods.

Around the same time, two spicy cuisines that had been established in America for centuries, Cajun and Southwestern (sometimes inaccurately called Mexican), began to be enjoyed far beyond Louisiana and New Mexico. American chefs were beginning to break free from the grip of French and Italian dominance and to explore the subcultures of their own country, resulting in dramatic new restaurants.

Meanwhile, chile pepper production and imports began to soar as demand grew. Chile pepper acreage doubled in New Mexico, Tabasco Sauce sales set new records, chili con carne cookoffs sprang up all over the country, and soon restaurants everywhere were serving fiery foods. At first, America's modern love affair with chile peppers looked like a fad, but now it has proven to be a definite trend.

In interviews conducted over the past few years, some of our Hot Spots chefs have expressed their views about the increasing popularity of chile peppers in both restaurant and home cuisines. In doing so, they sometimes waxed poetic about the pungent pods.

"Chiles are important because of their expressive qualities: they are more content than form," said Mark Miller of the Coyote Café in Santa Fe, New Mexico. "Therefore, they're not like cream and butter combinations. Chiles are more like jazz or a mariachi band—they're not bland, they hold their own. They don't lose their identity. The chiles add a liveliness to the food. It's pretty hard not to know you are eating chile items."

In a psychological vein, Miller continued: "Americans are feeling more comfortable about the eating experience. Eating chiles is fun; you can decide how hot you want a meal. Food that uses chiles is more appetite-stimulating and more satisfying. They raise your sensibilities. You cannot eat chiles and have a passive experience. It's food you become personally involved in. Chiles excite you. They unbridle your passions."

Paul Prudhomme, of K-Paul's in New Orleans, agrees. "Peppers can truly make you feel happy," he told us, "because when you eat a pepper, or something made with peppers, your taste buds get excited. Your brain gets the message that there's something special going on in your mouth, and—if it's very hot—that there's a possibility of danger. Peppers make eating more exciting and make the flavors of foods more pronounced."

Chris Schlesinger of the East Coast Grill in Cambridge, Massachusetts, discussed how long it has taken Americans to appreciate chiles. "Americans have awakened from a Rip Van Winkle sleep when it comes to enjoying fiery foods," he said. "America is one of the last countries to show a penchant for flavor in its food. The '80s were a learning decade for American palates.

Restaurants—along with their celebrity chefs—became quite popular. And Americans have finally discovered flavor, and the best flavor is chile flavor. People in this country are now aware that spice is good in food. They are no longer reluctant to try hot food. Palates are becoming aware of heat and can now pick out the different flavors even though there is heat. They've learned you can match the heat with accompanying strong flavors and have great tastes."

Stephan Pyles of the Routh Street Café in Dallas spoke of the health benefit of chiles. "With the intensity of chile flavors, I am finding that salt and fat are not needed to give great tastes to food. There is no doubt chile is becoming more and more mainstream in cooking throughout this country."

So, where will it all end? Will there be a fiery foods restaurant on every corner? Well, considering the popularity of Kentucky Fried Chicken's Hot and Spicy Wings, and the fact that McDonald's is now serving breakfast burritos, perhaps that idea is not so far-fetched after all. However, fast food restaurants will never serve up the wonderful recipes created by the chefs in this book!

A Pepper Primer

Here is the basic information regarding the chile peppers used in the recipes in this book. For more details, consult *The Whole Chile Pepper Book* (Little, Brown & Co., 1990) by Dave DeWitt and Nancy Gerlach, *The Great Chile Book* (Ten Speed Press, 1991) by Mark Miller, and *Peppers, The Domesticated Capsicums* (University of Texas Press, 1984) by Jean Andrews.

Ancho. Spanish for "wide," these chiles are the dried form of the poblano chile. They are about three inches wide and four inches long. The ancho has both the color and aroma of raisins, and for this reason is called, confusingly, pasilla ("little raisin") in

California. It is found in supermarkets in the Southwest and through the mail in other areas. Substitute: pasilla.

Cayenne. Legend holds that cayenne is the hottest pepper of them all, but it's not. However, it is hot enough to get everyone's attention when it's used in its commonest form—a powder. It is a favorite in African and Cajun dishes. Cayennes are about a half-inch to one inch wide and six to ten inches long. The pods are available through mail-order companies, and the powder can be found in the spice section in the supermarket. Substitute: piquin.

Chipotle. See Jalapeño.

Habanero. "From Havana" is the name of the hottest chile in the world, though there is some doubt that it originated there. Grown in the Caribbean (where it is called "Scotch bonnet"), the Yucatan Peninsula, and now in California and Texas, the Habanero is not only the most pungent pepper, it also has a unique, fruity, apricot-like aroma that is never forgotten. It is about an inch wide and an inch-and-a-half long. It is occasionally available fresh in supermarkets, in its pickled form in Caribbean stores, and now in dried form in some supermarkets and by mail order. Substitute: none for flavor, fresh piquins for heat.

Jalapeño. The "state pepper" of Texas, jalapeños may well be the most famous chiles in the world. They are certainly one of the most popular, with over 40,000 acres cultivated in Mexico alone. The medium-hot pods are about an inch wide and two inches long. Jalapeños are available fresh in supermarkets all over the country and can be found canned in water or pickled in vinegar or escabeche with other vegetables. Substitute: serrano. Smoked jalapeños are called *chipotles* and are available in dried form from mail order companies or canned in adobo sauce in the Mexican sections of supermarkets. Substitute: none.

New Mexican.   Formerly misnamed *Anaheim,* these fairly mild, long green chiles were grown for centuries in New Mexico before they were transplanted to California. They are the *de facto* New Mexico state symbol, with their image plastered over t-shirts, note cards, coffee mugs, and even underpants. These are the principal peppers used in the American versions of Mexican cooking. The pods are about two inches wide and six inches long. In green form, the pods are roasted over charcoal until the skins blister, and then are placed in a plastic bag to steam them. The skins are then removed and the chiles—sometimes seeded—are ready for use in recipes. Fresh New Mexican chiles are available in New Mexico, west Texas, and Arizona in August and September and from some mail-order companies. California Anaheim varieties are milder but are available in supermarkets all over the country. In the red form, the pods are available in supermarkets in the Southwest and from mail-order companies. The red pods are ground into powders ranging from crushed flakes to very fine; the powders are available from mail-order companies. Substitute: poblano for green, pasilla or ancho for red.

Pasilla.   This long, thin chile is generally found dried. Like the ancho, it evokes raisins; its name means "little raisin" in Spanish. The fairly mild pasilla was the immediate predecessor of the New Mexican variety. Because of its unique flavor, it is a favorite of Mexican *moleros,* cooks who specialize in *mole* sauces. The pods are about an inch wide and six or seven inches long. The pods, and powders made from the pods, are found in supermarkets in the Southwest and from mail-order companies. Substitute: ancho.

Piquin.   Also called *pequin, chilipiquin,* and *chiltepin* in its wild form, this variety has pods that vary in size from the head of a hatpin to two inches long. All are extremely hot, and aficionados, usually Texans, carry the small round ones in pillboxes just in case they accidentally encounter any bland food. They are available in grocery stores in the Southwest and from mail order companies. Substitute: cayenne and Oriental chiles such as santakas.

Poblano. The fresh green form of the ancho, the mild and tasty poblano is a favorite for stuffing because of its wide body. The pods measure about three inches wide by four inches long in a slightly conical shape. Like the New Mexican variety, the poblanos are also roasted and peeled before use. Poblanos are available fresh in supermarkets in the Southwest and in some specialty shops in other places. Substitute: New Mexican or, in chopped form, bell peppers mixed half and half with New Mexican.

Serrano. Meaning "from the mountains" in Spanish, the medium-hot serranos are the chile of choice for fresh salsas. In fact, in Mexico, fully ninety percent of the crop is used fresh, rather than being processed. The pods are about a half-inch wide and two inches long. *Serranos en escabeche,* serranos pickled with carrots and onions, is a popular canned snack in Mexico and the Southwestern United States and can be found in the Mexican food section of supermarkets. Substitute: jalapeños.

Other Ingredients

- **Chile Pastes.** These extremely hot condiments are usually found in Asian grocery stores. They combine extremely hot chiles with garlic, cooking oil, and a wide variety of spices. A rough approximation can be created by pureeing together the hottest red chile pods you can find with cloves of garlic, salt, and other spices you like such as cumin, ginger, allspice, or nutmeg.
- **Chile Oils.** Steep hot chile peppers in oil and you have chile oil, which can be used in place of cooking oil and even to spice up

popcorn. They are available in specialty shops and through mail-order companies.

- **Fish Sauce.**   Called *nuac nam* in Vietnam and *nam pla* in Thailand, this sauce usually combines chiles, fermented fish, lime, sugar, and garlic. It is available in Asian grocery stores.
- **Hot Sauces.**   More than a thousand hot sauces are manufactured all over the world. They range from red chiles in vinegar to combinations of chiles and vegetables. In this book, the term refers to any liquid hot sauce such as those made from Tabasco or Habanero chiles. They are available in supermarkets and from mail-order companies.
- **Garam Masala.**   A blend of dry-roasted, ground spices, this ingredient is similar to curry powder. If unavailable, an approximation can be made by grinding together dried hot chiles, black pepper, cinnamon, cloves, coriander, cumin, mace, nutmeg, and cardamom.

Mail-Order Sources

Dried chiles, spices, chile sauces, canned chiles, and fresh green New Mexican chiles in season: Old Southwest Trading Company, P.O. Box 7545, Albuquerque, NM 87194, (505) 836-0168.

Cajun products: K-Paul's Magic Seasoning Blends, P.O. Box 770034, New Orleans, LA 70177-0034.

Chile seeds: Shepherd's Garden Seeds, 6116 Highway 9, Felton, CA 95018, (408) 335-5311.

Fresh chiles: to find the nearest source for fresh jalapeños, serranos, and Habaneros, call Frieda's Finest, (213) 627-2981.

Hot sauces: Spectacular Sauces, P.O. Box 30010, Alexandria, VA 22310, (800) 999-4949.

Books and additional information: *Chile Pepper* magazine, P.O. Box 4278, Albuquerque, NM 87196, (800) 359-1483. (Bimonthly subscription, $15.95/year.)

Appealing Appetizers

Creative restaurant chefs have expanded the definition of the appetizer considerably. Originally, appetizers or hors d'oeuvre were finger food served in bite-sized portions to whet the appetite, not eliminate it. Prosper Montagné, writing in *Larousse Gastronomique,* advised that hors d'oeuvre "should be light and very delicate," especially when served before a meal of many courses.

These days, appetizers are often so rich and complex that they rival the other courses, and often diners mix and match several appetizers and skip the entrees and accompaniments of the meal entirely. This technique is often used at tapas bars; unfortunately, most tapas are not hot and spicy.

So, the definition of appetizers for this book relies on the tried and true method known as passing the buck. If the dish appears on the restaurant menu as an appetizer, an appetizer it is. The recipes are arranged roughly in the order of their complexity, starting simply and finishing with some rather elaborate creations.

CANTINA CHILE CON QUESO
The Cantina, Raleigh, North Carolina

Tim Forsman and John Kennedy of The Cantina have a simple philosophy when it comes to hot and spicy food. They believe in cooking the food spicy enough so the customers will order another beer, but mild enough so they will crave another helping. At their Tex-Mex restaurant on the main "strip" of North Carolina State University, they balance the heat with plenty of flavor, as this dish proves. Chile con Queso can be served as a dip for tostada chips, as a sauce for topping hamburgers, or even as a thick soup.

1 **cup fresh jalapeños,** stems removed, seeded, and chopped

3 medium onions, quartered

2 pounds fresh tomatoes, quartered

¼ cup vegetable oil

5 pounds sliced American cheese

1 pound grated cheddar cheese

6 medium eggs, beaten

1 Tablespoon chicken base

Boil the jalapeños in 2 quarts of water for 5 minutes. Add the tomatoes and onions and boil for 10 minutes. Drain the vegetables and retain 3 cups of water. In a blender, blend the vegetables and the retained water on the lowest speed for 5 to 7 seconds.

Sauté this puree in the oil over medium heat for 90 seconds. Lower the heat and add the American cheese one slice at a time, allowing it to melt slowly, stirring constantly.

Add the cheddar cheese and stir until completely melted. Add the eggs mixed with the chicken base and cook for 5 minutes, stirring constantly.

Serves: 12 or more as a dip
Heat Scale: Medium

"BALD EAGLE" WINGS AND DRUMS
The Crazy Flamingo, Marco Island, Florida

This raw bar and seafood grill serves the hottest chicken wings in the country, according to owner Anthony Rainone. He should know, since he's been eating hot peppers since he was three years old. His philosophy of fiery foods is that "you can't cook hot if you can't eat hot." He also notes: "Hot is easy, but hot with real *flavor* is the key."

¼ **cup freshly ground Habanero chile**

6 **Tablespoons hot sauce such as Durkee's**

10 **Tablespoons Matouk's West Indies Flambeau sauce,** or substitute another Habanero-based sauce

2 **Tablespoons cayenne powder**

6 chicken wings (tips removed) and 6 chicken drumsticks

peanut oil for deep frying

celery sticks and blue cheese dressing for garnish

Mix together the first four ingredients to make a sauce.

Place the wings and drums in a basket in the deep fryer and cook until the wings begin to float. Place a second basket on top of the chicken and cook for 2 more minutes. Remove and shake off extra oil.

Toss the chicken in the sauce until fully coated. Serve with the celery sticks and blue cheese dressing.

Serves: 8 to 10
Heat Scale: Extremely Hot

CRAB-STUFFED JALAPEÑOS
Great Jones Café, New York, New York

According to owner Jim Moffett, this small restaurant and bar in Manhattan is popular for three reasons: good, cheap Cajun and homestyle cooking, a fun bar, and an award-winning jukebox. He says, "All of these elements come together in a bustling, convivial environment, fueled by super-hot Cajun martinis!" The recipe below, by head chef Mark Hitzges, is similar to the popular Mexican snacks, tuna-stuffed jalapeños.

1 pound crabmeat
½ cup chopped cilantro
1 heart celery, finely chopped
¼ cup fresh lime juice
2 Tablespoons olive oil
2 eggs, slightly beaten
1 clove minced garlic

salt and **cayenne powder to taste**
10 **large jalapeños,** roasted, peeled, seeds removed through a small hole cut where the stem was
oil for deep frying

Combine all the ingredients except the oil and jalapeños and mix well. Stuff the crabmeat mixture into the jalapeños. Deep fry for about 3 minutes, drain, and serve hot.

Serves: 5 to 10
Heat Scale: Hot

BRICK ALLEY NACHOS

Brick Alley Pub and Restaurant, Newport, Rhode Island

This lively watering hole offers its clientele fifteen different hot sauces with varying degrees of heat. Some of the sauces, such as the one below, are served over owner/chef Ralph Plumb's nachos, which have been voted the best in Rhode Island.

2	**jalapeños,** stems removed, seeded, and chopped	½	teaspooon dried oregano
2	cups tomato puree	¾	teaspoon freshly ground black pepper
1	green onion, finely chopped	½	teaspoon minced fresh garlic
1	Tablespoon minced fresh cilantro	1-½	pounds cheddar cheese
		1	pound tostada chips

To make the sauce, combine the first 7 ingredients, mix well, and keep at room temperature.

Melt the cheese in a double boiler.

To serve, place equal portions of chips on plates or in bowls. Pour cheese over the chips and top with the sauce.

Serves: 4
Heat Scale: Medium

〰〰〰〰〰

CAJUN MUSHROOMS

Mildred's VIP Catering, Jackson, Mississippi

Owner Mildred Brown attended the Julia Child Cooking School, was a chef at the Pallette restaurant, owned Mildred's Tea Room, and then decided that catering was the answer to her entrepreneurial goals. As her friend Phyllis Spiegel describes her: "She has become the best caterer in

Mississippi and can handle thousands with a cool head." Well, her head may be cool, but her palate loves the hot stuff. These mushrooms can also be sliced and served over grilled steaks.

½ cup unsalted butter
1 pound fresh mushrooms, cleaned and trimmed
3 **Tablespoons jalapeños,** stems removed, seeded, and minced

4 Tablespoons Worcestershire sauce
1 teaspoon lemon juice
⅛ cup white wine

Sauté the mushrooms in butter for 3 minutes over medium heat. Add the remaining ingredients and simmer for an additional 2 minutes. Place mushrooms and sauce in a chafing dish and serve with toothpicks.

Serves: 4 to 6
Heat Scale: Medium

TOMAS' CHILE RAJAS CON QUESO
La Paz Restaurante Mexicano, Atlanta, Georgia

The original La Paz was opened in Atlanta in 1979 by Tom Nicoloff, who subsequently established branch restaurants in Charlotte, North Carolina, and Knoxville, Tennessee. Tom, a third-generation restaurateur, specializes in cooking Southwestern foods, such as this appetizer of roasted chile strips with cheese.

2 Tablespoons butter
½ **cup New Mexican green chiles,** stems removed, roasted, peeled, seeded, and cut into strips (*rajas*)
2 **serrano chiles,** stems removed, seeded, and diced
2 cloves garlic, diced

½ cup diced onions
½ cup diced fresh tomatoes
⅓ cup minced fresh cilantro
1 cup shredded Monterey Jack cheese
1 Tablespoon sour cream

Sauté the ingredients except the cheese and sour cream in the butter for 2 to 3 minutes. Sprinkle the cheese on top, cover, and cook over low heat for 30 seconds. Remove from the heat and allow to steam for 1 minute.

Pour the mixture into a bowl and top with the sour cream. Serve with fresh tostada chips for dipping.

Serves: 4
Heat Scale: Medium

〜〜〜〜〜〜〜〜〜〜

JALAPEÑO PATTY HOTS
The Pink Adobe, Santa Fe, New Mexico

One of the most famous restaurants in New Mexico, The Pink Adobe is over forty-five years old. However, the building it's in is even older—over three hundred years older, in fact. The classic adobe building has walls 36-inches thick and has six fireplaces. Owner and recipe creator Rosalea Murphy believes that some form of chile peppers is necessary to add a distinctive character to any dish. This appetizer also makes a nice lunch when served with a fresh fruit salad.

1 8-ounce can albacore chunk white tuna	⅛ cup chopped celery
2 cups cold mashed potatoes	⅛ cup onion
3 Tablespoons butter	1 egg, beaten
1 small fresh jalapeño chile, stem and seeds removed, minced	1 cup cracker crumbs made from saltines pulverized in a blender

Drain the tuna, break it into chunks, and mix with the mashed potatoes. Set aside.

Heat 1 tablespoon of the butter in a small skillet and add the jalapeño, celery, and onion. Sauté until the onion is soft. Add this to the potato-tuna mixture, stir in the egg, and form the mixture into eight patties.

Roll the patties in the cracker crumbs and chill them in the refrigerator for about 30 minutes.

Heat the remaining butter in a large skillet and fry the patties until brown on both sides. Drain and serve.

Serves: 8 as an appetizer
Heat Scale: Mild

〰〰〰〰〰〰〰〰〰〰〰

THAI COCONUT GINGER SHRIMP
On the Verandah, Highlands, North Carolina

A "speakeasy" in the 1930s, On the Verandah is now a rustic restaurant that overlooks Lake Sequoyah in the southern Blue Ridge Mountains. During the summer, guests love to sit out on the 50-seat veranda and enjoy the lake view while dining. The menu reflects the interest of owners Alan and Marta Figel in spicy international cuisine, including this unusual appetizer.

4 Tablespoons Louisiana-style hot sauce

1 15-ounce can coconut cream

3 Tablespoons Thai fish sauce

3 Tablespoons minced ginger

1 Tablespoon white pepper

16 jumbo shrimp, peeled and deveined

4 Tablespoons grated shallots

4 Tablespoons grated lemon peel

4 Tablespoons vegetable oil

Combine the first 5 ingredients for a sauce and set aside.

Sauté the shrimp, shallots, and lemon peel in the oil on high heat for 3 minutes until the shrimp is lightly browned. Add the sauce and cook until reduced, not more than 4 minutes. Serve with a salad of bok choy and sliced scallions over mixed greens.

Serves: 4
Heat Scale: Medium

wwwwwwwwww

CHA GIO (VIETNAMESE EGGROLLS)
East Wind Restaurant, Alexandria, Virginia

Khai Nguyen of the East Wind points out that Vietnamese restaurants now outnumber Chinese restaurants in Paris, proof that this cuisine is finally being recognized for its excellence. The following recipe is from head chef Thuan, who is from central Vietnam.

3 onions, minced
¼ pound ground cooked shrimp
¼ pound shredded cooked crabmeat
¼ pound ground cooked chicken breast
¼ pound ground cooked pork
¼ pound minced carrot
¼ pound minced cabbage
1 clove garlic, minced

1 ounce cellophane noodles, soaked in warm water for 20 minutes, drained, and cut into 1-inch lengths
½ teaspoon black pepper
½ teaspoon salt
½ teaspoon sugar
20 sheets rice paper
peanut oil for deep frying
Vietnamese serrano hot sauce, such as Sriracha

Combine all ingredients in a bowl—except the hot sauce, rice paper, and oil—and mix well. Place the filling on the sheets of rice paper and wrap up one at a time.

Deep fry the rolls in the oil until golden brown. Serve with the hot sauce for dipping.

Yield: 20 eggrolls
Heat Scale: Varies

MANILA CLAMS IN RED CHILE BROTH
Coyote Café, Santa Fe, New Mexico

Chilehead chef Mark Miller of the Coyote Café developed and wrote "The Great Chile Posters" (Celestial Arts, 1990), a collection of botanically accurate, lifesize photographs of both fresh and dried chiles. We asked Mark why chile peppers have become so popular in cooking in recent years. "They are accessible, exciting, and not expensive," he said. "Chiles are fundamentally one of the greatest foods ever cultivated in terms of taste. Chiles are to food what the grape is to wine." And that about sums it up.

2 cups fresh clam broth (or 1 cup bottled clam juice and 1 cup water)

2 dried New Mexican red chiles, stemmed and seeded

4 Tablespoons extra virgin olive oil

4 cloves garlic, roasted and peeled

6 Roma tomatoes, roasted and coarsely chopped

48 Manila baby clams, scrubbed

Heat the clam broth till hot and soak the chiles in it until they are limp. Puree the mixture in a blender and set aside.

In one tablespoon of the olive oil, sauté the garlic and tomatoes. Add the clams, toss, and add the chile broth. Cover and steam until the clams open, about 3 minutes. Remove the clams and keep warm.

Add the remaining olive oil to the broth, stir, and boil the mixture for 30 seconds. Serve the clams in a bowl with the broth.

Serves: 4
Heat Scale: Mild to Medium

CREOLE CRAWFISH ENCHILADAS
Galley del Mar, Ridgeland, Mississippi

Here is a perfect example of a collision of cuisines. The Southwest meets the Deep South in this interesting combination of tastes and textures from the Galley del Mar in Mississippi.

1-½ cups minced onion	3 **canned chipotle chiles,** stems removed, seeded, and minced
½ cup minced bell pepper	
¼ cup clarified butter	½ cup grated Monterey Jack cheese
2 cups heavy cream	
4 ounces cream cheese, cut into cubes	½ **cup hot pepper cheese,** grated
½ teaspoon oregano	10 7-inch corn tortillas (or more until the filling runs out)
½ teaspoon salt	
½ teaspoon white pepper	
¼ teaspoon chopped cilantro	2 cups Creole Sauce (see recipe)
¼ teaspoon cumin	
¼ cup chopped scallions	1-½ cups grated mozzarella cheese
½ pound crawfish tails with fat	

Sauté the onion and bell pepper in the butter until the onion becomes translucent. Add the cream and cream cheese and simmer 10 minutes. Add all spices, scallions, the crawfish tails, and chipotles. Remove from the heat and stir in the grated cheeses. Refrigerate this mixture until it becomes firm.

Fry each corn tortilla in hot oil for a few seconds each side until it is softened. Drain on paper towels. Spoon two tablespoons of the mixture onto each tortilla and roll it up. Place each enchilada in a ramekin, seam side down, and spoon Creole Sauce over the top. Add the mozzarella and broil until bubbly hot.

Serves: 10 or more

Heat Scale: Medium

CREOLE SAUCE

½ **teaspoon cayenne powder**	3 shallots, minced
4 large tomatoes, peeled, seeded, and chopped	1 sprig each fresh thyme and parsley
1 bell pepper, chopped	1 Tablespoon flour
1 teaspoon butter	1 Tablespoon butter
2 cloves garlic, minced	1 cup sherry

Boil together the first 7 ingredients in 2 cups of water for 20 minutes. Remove from the heat and mash through a sieve.

Make a roux with the butter and flour, and when the roux is brown add the strained tomato sauce. Stir and simmer for 5 minutes. Add the sherry and simmer until the sauce thickens, about 20 minutes.

Yield: About 2 cups
Heat Scale: Mild

wwwwwwwww

CAJUN CAVIAR

Bayou Bar and Grill, San Diego, California

The Bayou is the fifth Creole/Cajun-style restaurant that owners Bud Deslatte and Les Carloss have opened during the past thirteen years. The others are located in New Orleans and Atlanta. Bud, who also creates the recipes, noted that the restaurants feature "casual dining with contemporary and upbeat ambience." Part of the upbeat ambience is the use of hot and spicy ingredients. This recipe is designed to serve a large party.

1 pound butter

3 Tablespoons Creole seasoning containing cayenne

1 pound crawfish tails, cleaned

1 pound shrimp, peeled, deveined, tails removed

2 yellow onions, quartered

5 sticks celery, chopped

3 bell peppers, seeded and chopped

3 Tablespoons garlic, pureed

3 Tablespoons basil

2 Tablespoons thyme

3 Tablespoons tomato paste

3 Tablespoons Worcestershire sauce

4 Tablespoons white flour

2 cups green onions, finely chopped

salt to taste

1 Tablespoon Louisiana hot sauce, or more to taste

French bread slices cut ½ inch thick and allowed to stale overnight

2 cups garlic butter

Melt 1 stick of butter in a skillet to sizzling, add 1 tablespoon of Creole seasoning and the crawfish tails and sauté on high heat for 3 or 4 minutes. Remove the crawfish, add another stick of butter, allow it to sizzle, and add the shrimp. Sauté on high heat for 4 to 5 minutes and remove from pan. Reserve the juices in the skillet.

Place the crawfish and shrimp in a food processor and pulse to fine (do not puree).

Place the onion, celery, and bell peppers in the processor and pulse to fine (do not puree). Put the processed vegetables in a sieve and squeeze the excess water from them.

In the original skillet, add 2 sticks of butter and bring to sizzling. Add the processed onion mixture and the remaining Creole seasoning and sauté on high heat for 5 minutes, stirring constantly. Reduce the heat and add the garlic, basil, and thyme and cook for 5 minutes more.

Add the cooked, processed seafood and the tomato paste, Worcestershire, and the flour. Cook over medium heat for 5 minutes, stirring constantly. Add the green onions, salt, and hot sauce and cook for yet another 5 minutes.

To serve, brush the bread slices with garlic butter and spread the warm "caviar" mixture on top.

Serves: At least 20

Heat Scale: Medium, but varies up

BRAISED LAMB FRANKIE
The Bombay Café, Los Angeles, California

Voted the best Indian restaurant in Los Angeles by *Los Angeles Magazine,* the Bombay Café emphasizes unusual and "non-clichéd" Indian dishes, and features chutneys rather than curries. Chef Neela Paniz strives to re-create home-style, traditional Indian food, which of course must contain chiles. "They should never dominate a dish completely as to obliterate all other flavors," she says, "but neither should they be skimped on for fear of their heat." Lamb Frankie is an Indian "burrito" that is popular at Candy Beach in Bombay.

4	Tablespoons corn oil	**2**	**Tablespoons cayenne powder**
2	medium onions, thinly sliced	2	medium tomatoes, sliced
6	cloves garlic, pureed in a blender	1	1-inch piece of ginger, julienned
1	2-inch piece of ginger, peeled and pureed in a blender	**8**	**to 12 serrano chiles** (or other small, fresh green chiles), stems removed, seeded, and cut in half lengthwise
2	pounds of cubed, boneless lamb leg meat		salt to taste
2-½	Tablespoons coriander powder		fresh cilantro for garnish
2-½	Tablespoons cumin powder		Indian soft *nan* bread or substitute pita bread
¼	teaspoon turmeric		

Heat the corn oil on high, add the onions, reduce the heat, and sauté on medium heat until they are dark brown. Add the pureed garlic and ginger and cook for 1 minute. Add the lamb and dry spices and sauté until the lamb is brown (about 15 minutes), stirring constantly and taking care not to burn the lamb or spices.

Add the tomatoes, julienned ginger, and chiles, reduce the heat, and simmer until the lamb is tender. Adjust for salt, garnish with cilantro, and serve wrapped in the *nan* bread or in pita pockets.

Serves: 8 as an appetizer
Heat Scale: Hot

ZIA'S BLUE CORN FLAUTAS
Zia Café, Santa Barbara, California

The foods of New Mexico now appear in restaurants all over the country. In Santa Barbara, they are re-created (with local innovations) at the Zia Café, which is owned by Elena and David Campos. The word "flauta" means "flute" in Spanish, an allusion to the rolled shape of the tortillas in this dish.

1 pound ground beef
½ **cup New Mexican green chiles,** chopped
1 red bell pepper, seeds removed, julienned
1 yellow bell pepper, seeds removed, julienned
1 onion, thinly sliced
½ teaspoon salt
¼ teaspoon cumin

12 blue corn tortillas
   vegetable oil for frying
1 cup shredded lettuce
2 **cups of your favorite salsa**
2 cups grated cheddar cheese
1 cup guacamole (see recipe, page 145)
1 cup chopped tomatoes

Brown the beef in a skillet and drain the excess fat. Add the chiles, bell peppers, onions, salt, and cumin, and cook until the onions and bell peppers are soft.

Fry the tortillas in the oil for a few seconds until soft. Remove and drain on paper towels. Place the beef mixture in the center of the tortillas, roll them up, and secure with toothpicks. Fry the flautas in oil until crisp.

Place the lettuce on plates, place two flautas on top, and top with the salsa, cheese, guacamole, and tomatoes.

Serves: 6
Heat Scale: Medium

SHRIMP AND SMOKED CHEDDAR
FLAUTAS WITH HOT ORANGE SALSA
La Casa Sena, Santa Fe, New Mexico

Chef Kip McClerin supervises six different menus at La Casa Sena, which keeps him experimenting with many variations on the theme of hot and spicy. Here is his "flute" variation, a recipe which illustrates how innovative chefs are taking "peasant food" (as all ethnic cuisines have been labeled for years) and elevating it to new heights.

BASIL PESTO MARINADE

2	cups fresh basil	½	cup olive oil
2	ounces sun-dried tomatoes	⅓	cup piñon nuts, toasted
1	Tablespoon minced garlic		salt and pepper to taste

Blend all ingredients in a food processor until finely minced.

Yield: 1 cup

HOT ORANGE SALSA

6	**small, hot, dried chiles** (such as piquins or chiltepins), stems removed	4	scallions, minced, white part only
		1	pint heavy cream
2	**pinches red chile powder** juice of 1 orange	½	teaspoon tomato paste salt to taste
2	Tablespoons white wine		honey (optional)

Combine all ingredients except honey and simmer until the chiles swell up and the cream thickens. Drizzle honey lightly into the sauce if desired.

Yield: 2 cups
Heat Scale: Medium

THE FLAUTAS

10 medium shrimp, peeled,
    deveined, tails removed
½ red bell pepper, seeded and
    julienned
½ green bell pepper, seeded and
    julienned
½ yellow bell pepper, seeded
    and julienned

3 scallions, julienned
2 cups grated smoked cheddar
    cheese
4 flour tortillas
    vegetable oil for deep frying

Marinate the shrimp in the pesto for at least 4 hours.

Sauté the shrimp and pesto together for three minutes, then remove from heat and cut each shrimp into 3 or 4 pieces.

Divide the shrimp mixture into quarters and spread on the edge of each tortilla. Add the remaining ingredients in equal proportions, and roll up, securing with toothpicks.

Deep-fry the flautas in oil until golden brown, about 3 to 5 minutes. Remove the flautas and drain. Remove the toothpick, cut the flautas in half on the plate, and serve topped with the orange salsa.

Serves: 4
Heat Scale: Varies with the amount of salsa added

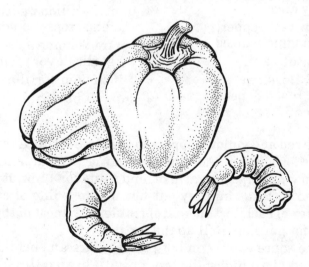

DUNGENESS CRAB ENCHILADAS
Campton Place Hotel, San Francisco, California

Jan Birnbaum, executive chef at the Campton Place, prepares contemporary American cuisine, combining "American techniques from several regions of experience to create aggressively flavored, exciting dishes." Here, enchiladas are transformed into a spicy seafood appetizer.

THE SAUCE

1 **poblano chile,** stem removed, roasted, peeled, and seeded

8 tomatillos

⅛ bunch fresh cilantro

2 Tablespoons lime juice

10 spinach leaves

salt and pepper to taste

Place all ingredients in a blender and blend until smooth.

THE ENCHILADAS

1 small red bell pepper, seeded and finely diced

1 small yellow bell pepper, seeded and finely diced

2 Tablespoons olive oil

1 **poblano chile,** stem removed, roasted, peeled, and seeded

12 ounces dungeness crab meat

½ bunch scallions, sliced thin on a bias, tops included

1 pound Sonoma Jack cheese, garlic flavor preferred

6 6-inch flour tortillas

¼ cup soft butter

Sauté ¾ of the red and yellow peppers in the olive oil until soft, reserving the remainder for garnish. Add the poblano, crab meat, and most of the scallions, reserving some for garnish, and sauté for 1 minute. Reserve.

Butter the tortillas and lay out flat. Make a line of crab mixture down the center of each tortilla and sprinkle with most of the cheese, reserving some for garnish. Roll up the tortillas.

Divide the sauce evenly on hot plates. Place an enchilada on each, seam down, and place under the broiler until heated through. Remove, sprinkle with the remaining cheese, and garnish with the remaining bell peppers and scallions. Serve immediately.

Serves: 6
Heat Scale: Mild

〜〜〜〜〜〜〜〜〜〜〜〜

GRILLED BLUEFISH WITH CHIPOTLE VINAIGRETTE
East Coast Grill, Cambridge, Massachusetts

Chris Schlesinger, chef and owner of the East Coast Grill, describes this recipe, which calls for pungency in every manner:

"Here you're talking strength against strength—a very strong, distinctive-tasting, oily fish versus a hot, smoky, highly acidic vinaigrette. A great combination, as both flavors will definitely be heard from. I like to use the chipotle chile a lot with grilled food, because the tastes complement each other very well, and because it is always available canned.

"This dish can be served warm or cold, and is a good item for buffets because the cooling-down process doesn't affect the flavors. If you want to make a more colorful presentation, throw a couple of lime halves on the platter and sprinkle the fish with chopped cilantro and raw red onion."

1 **Tablespoon pureed chipotle chile**
1 teaspoon chopped cilantro
4 Tablespoons cider vinegar
1 Tablespoon brown prepared mustard
   juice of 2 limes

1 teaspoon sugar
½ cup virgin olive oil
   salt and freshly cracked black pepper to taste
2 8-ounce bluefish fillets
2 Tablespoons vegetable oil

In a small bowl, whisk together the chipotle chile, cilantro, vinegar, mustard, lime juice, and sugar. Add the olive oil, whisking, until well mixed. Add salt and pepper to taste.

Season the fish with salt and pepper and rub with the vegetable oil.
Over medium-low heat, place the fillets skin side up on the grill, covered with a pie pan. Cook 10 to 12 minutes, remove the pie pan, and flip with a spatula. Cook an additional 5 minutes. Check to see if it's completely done by probing the flesh, looking for consistent opacity.

Remove the fish from the grill, place on a platter, cut into appetizer portions, and pour the prepared sauce over it.

Serves: 4
Heat Scale: Medium

wwwwwwwwww

SIZZLING CRAB EMPANADAS
WITH SALSA DIABLO

Silverheels Southwest Grill,
Silverthorne, Colorado

Owner and chef Robert Starekow, who started cooking at an early age (he was an entrant in the Betty Crocker Bake-Off at the age of eight), prepares some of the food at Silverheels "via Stone Age cookery on fiery hot granite slabs at the table." That ought to get the diners' attention! He believes in using hot chiles as "an exciter for the palate, with an underlying sense of warmth that enhances the delicate flavor of our dishes."

5 ounces cream cheese at room temperature

2 cups pepper Monterey Jack cheese, grated

2 eggs, beaten

2 **serrano chiles,** stems removed, seeded, and minced

1 pound shredded snow crab meat

2 Tablespoons minced onion

1 teaspoon minced garlic

1 teaspoon ground cumin

2 teaspoons ground coriander

50 wonton wrappers, or more
    vegetable oil for deep frying

Mix the cream cheese and jack cheese in a large mixing bowl. Add the eggs and mix until the mixture is creamy. Add the remaining ingredients except the wrappers and oil and mix well, taking care not to pulverize the crab.

Fill a pastry bag (use no tip) with the mixture and set aside. Lay out the wonton wrappers and mist them with a spray bottle of water. Using the pastry bag, place about a rounded teaspoon of the mixture on each of 25 wonton wrappers, or more. Mist the wrappers again and place another wrapper on top of each mixture-filled wrapper. Press the top wrapper around the filling to seal and mist again. Fold the four corners of each empanada into the center and pinch to seal. Place them in a freezer and freeze solidly.

Deep fry the frozen empanadas in oil until deep golden and puffed. Serve with the Salsa Diablo for dipping.

Yield: 25 empanadas
Heat Scale: Mild

SALSA DIABLO

2 serrano chiles, stems removed, seeded, and minced

1 cup orange marmalade

½ cup crushed pineapple

2 cups apple jelly

2 Tablespoons prepared horseradish

1 teaspoon powdered mustard

1 teaspoon black pepper

In a blender on low speed, mix the first four ingredients. Pour into a bowl, mix in the remaining ingredients, and allow to sit at least an hour before serving.

Yield: 2-½ cups
Heat Scale: Medium

CHILE RELLENO TART
WITH MONTRACHET CUSTARD
The Santa Fe Café, Seattle, Washington

The restaurant that offers this recipe is so named because owners Greg and Steve Gibbons grew up in New Mexico. The Santa Fe Café features traditional food of that state along with innovations that incorporate many native ingredients. The three-step process in this recipe is well worth the effort, and this remarkable appetizer could also be served as a dessert.

BLUE CORN PASTRY

¾ cup blue corn meal
1 teaspoon salt
1 cup flour
12 Tablespoons butter, cut into
¼-inch cubes

1 Tablespoon Montrachet Custard (see recipe)
4 Tablespoons ice-cold water

Mix all the dry ingredients and place them in a food processor equipped with a plastic pastry blade. With the food processor running, drop the butter in swiftly, piece by piece. Add the 1 tablespoon custard. Do not overblend. Open the processor bowl and mix with a spoon. Re-cover it, and, with the processor running, add the ice water one tablespoon at a time. Allow the processor to run until the pastry balls up and runs cleanly around the bowl. Remove the pastry and shape into a sphere. Flatten it carefully on plastic wrap, cover, and refrigerate for 30 minutes.

Roll out on a floured surface and place in a 12-inch tart pan with a lightly buttered bottom. Do not butter the sides. Line with aluminum foil, weight with baking ballast (dry beans work well) and bake for 15 minutes in a 375 degree oven.

MONTRACHET CUSTARD

4 eggs
¾ cup whipping cream
3 ounces Montrachet cheese at room temperature

4 Tablespoons butter at room temperature

Place all ingredients in a food processor and blend until all the cheese and butter are incorporated.

THE TART

¾ pound grated Gruyère cheese
¾ pound grated mozzarella
    cheese
    Blue Corn Pastry

**2 cups New Mexican cooked
    and minced green chile**
    Montrachet Custard
¼ cup grated Colby cheese

Sprinkle the Gruyère and mozzarella on the Blue Corn Pastry, top with the green chile, and pour on the Montrachet Custard. Scatter the Colby over the top.

Bake for 40 minutes in a 375 degree oven, or until golden brown. The center should bounce back when touched.

Serves: 8
Heat Scale: Mild to Medium

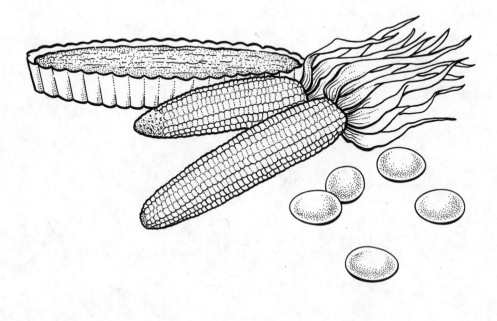

Spicy Salsas and Salads

Salsas and sauces are the foundation of hot and spicy cuisines from Mexico to India to Thailand. Although the Spanish word "salsa" translates as "sauce" in English, the two words are now used to describe two entirely different techniques. Salsas are uncooked and sauces are cooked—it's that simple. Salsas are used with tostada chips as an appetizer or are served over grilled, roasted, or broiled meats, poultry, and seafood. Sauces also are used as toppings, but more commonly they form the basis of combination dishes from casseroles to curries.

James Beard once claimed that salads did not come into use until the late nineteenth century. Apparently he missed the Roman epigrammist Martial's discussion of whether salads were better at the beginning or end of a meal. In America, salads have been around since the first colonists raised greens of all kinds, but occasionally they have been much maligned. Food writers John and Karen Hess, in their book, *The Taste of America,* believe this is because supermarket produce such as "iceberg lettuce and cotton tomatoes have driven tasty greens and real tomatoes from the market," and add that commercial dressings haven't helped either.

Leave it to innovative chefs to rescue salads and turn them from a few leaves of lettuce, a couple of hard tomatoes, and a commercial French dressing into elaborate affairs combining many diverse ingredients. Who would have dared to add chile peppers or meats to salads in the '50s and '60s? It was unthinkable then, but it's fashionable now.

We begin this chapter with a profusion of fresh salsas, follow them with some tasty cooked sauces, and wind up with a collection of eclectic salads.

EL TORITO SALSA FRESCA
El Torito Restaurants, Irvine, California

What better way to start the salsas and salads than with a classic Mexican salsa fresca? This salsa is also called *salsa cruda, pico de gallo,* and numerous other names. El Torito Restaurants began operation in Encino, California, in 1954 and now have 177 operations in twenty-six states. They employ three executive chefs who work on nothing but new ideas and ways of improving the chain's food.

2 **Tablespoons jalapeños,** stems removed, seeded, and finely diced (or substitute serranos)
2 cups tomatoes diced ¼ inch
½ cup onion diced ¼ inch
1 Tablespoon vegetable oil
1 teaspoon white vinegar
1 teaspoon freshly squeezed lime juice
½ teaspoon dried Mexican oregano (leaf)
¼ teaspoon salt
¼ cup finely chopped cilantro leaves

Combine all ingredients, mix well, and allow to sit for an hour to blend flavors. Serve with tostada chips.

Yield: 3 cups
Heat Scale: Medium

〰〰〰〰〰

FRESH TOMATO-PEACH SALSA
Piñon Grill, Inn at McCormick Ranch, Scottsdale, Arizona

The Piñon Grill specializes in distinctive Southwestern cuisine and overlooks Camelback Lake and the majestic McDowell Mountains. Executive Chef Farn Boggie, who hails from the Cavendish Hotel in London, where he cooked for such notables as Queen Elizabeth and Prince Philip, seems to have adjusted quite well to the Southwest, as evidenced by his culinary creations.

1 **red serrano chile,** stem removed, seeded, and minced (or more, to taste)
1 cup fresh tomato, minced
½ red onion, minced
2 Tablespoons fresh cilantro, chopped fine

1 Tablespoon fresh lime juice
1 Tablespoon olive oil
1 teaspoon salt
1 teaspoon brown sugar
1 fresh peach, peeled, pitted, and minced

Combine all ingredients and let stand for 1 hour. Serve this salsa with grilled meats, poultry, and seafood.

Yield: 2 cups
Heat Scale: Mild

~~~~~~~~~~~

XNIPEC SALSA

Pinch-a-Pollo Restaurant, Austin, Texas

This restaurant in Austin features achiote-marinated grilled chicken accompanied by the diner's choice of *sixteen* different hot sauces from mild to wild. This one's definitely wild. Xnipec, pronounced "SCHNEE-peck," is Mayan for "dog's breath" and features the hottest chile pepper in the world, the Habanero. Serve it with grilled poultry or fish.

juice of 4 limes
1 onion, red or purple preferred, diced

4 **Habanero chiles,** stems and seeds removed, diced
1 tomato, diced

Soak the diced onion in the lime juice for at least 30 minutes. Add the other ingredients and mix, salt to taste, and add a little water if desired.

Yield: 1-½ cups.
Heat Scale: Extremely Hot

QUACA-CHILE SALSA
El Norteño, Albuquerque, New Mexico

Leo Nuñez, owner of his family-run Mexican (note: *not* New Mexican) restaurant, says that his philosophy of food is simple: serve what no other Mexican restaurant in the United States is serving. By that he means the unique cuisine of northern Mexico, including such delicacies as *cabrito* (young goat) and *lengua* (cow's tongue). To spice up such entrees, he serves this salsa.

3   or more serrano chiles,
    stems removed and seeded
2   medium tomatoes, chopped
¼   cup chopped white onion
1   clove garlic

⅛   cup chopped cilantro
1   whole ripe avocado, peeled
    and pitted
¼   cup water

Combine all ingredients in a blender with enough water to make a smooth sauce—not quite thick, not quite thin. The salsa should stick to chips enough to give a good taste, but should be thinner than guacamole. Serve with tostada chips or as an unusual accompaniment to meats, poultry, and seafood.

Serves: 4
Heat Scale: Medium

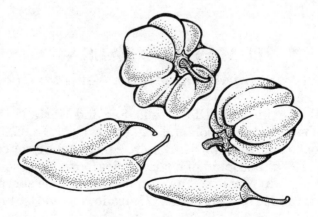

RAUL'S SALSA

JJ & Company, San Rafael, California

The two initials in the name of this casual restaurant stand for Jim and Jeff Durkin, the owners. The chef, Raul Luvian, is from Jalisco, Mexico, and prepares recipes handed down from his grandparents. Here is his version of a classic Mexican *pico de gallo* salsa.

10	serrano chiles, stems removed, seeded, and pureed	½	bunch cilantro, chopped
3	cups tomato juice	2	tomatoes, chopped fine
½	cup water	1	Tablespoon garlic powder
½	onion, chopped fine	1	teaspoon salt
		1	teaspoon white pepper

Mix all ingredients together and let them sit for 1 hour. Serve with tostada chips.

Yield: 1 quart
Heat Scale: Hot

TOMATILLO SALSA

El Norteño, Albuquerque, New Mexico

Everyone gets into the act at El Norteño. Leo and Marta Nuñez are proprietors and chefs, and their son and daughters (Leo, Jr., Gabriella, and Yvette) are cooks and waiters. They were somewhat disconcerted when asked about their "philosophy" of hot and spicy foods, since such foods are ordinary table fare in Mexico. This simple salsa can be served with tostada chips, or as an ingredient in their Guisado Norteño (see recipe, page 83).

5   **serrano chiles,** or more to
    taste, chopped
½   pound tomatillos, husks
    removed, chopped

½   cup white onion, chopped
1   Tablespoon cilantro, chopped
¼   teaspoon salt

Place all ingredients in a blender and puree, adding just enough water to make a "gravy."

Serves: 4
Heat Scale: Medium

~~~~~~~~~~~~~~~~~~

RIVERWOOD DEATH SAUCE
The Riverwood, Boone, North Carolina

As described by owners Randy Plachy and Sara Littlejohn, The Riverwood "has a warm, mountainy kind of ambience." But the food is more than just warm, it's downright hot. Randy believes that "spicy food should kick some butt" and says he knows he has succeeded when the food is so hot it "burns both tongue and cheek." His and the sous-chef J. Alton Terry's Death Sauce is a perfect example of this philosophy. It can be used as a condiment to spice up any dish.

1   **fistful of dried piquin
    chiles,** or substitute
    "Chinese" chiles, chile de
    árbol, mirasols, or santakas
1   **Tablespoon Louisiana hot
    sauce**
½   **teaspoon cayenne powder**
1   teaspoon mushroom soy sauce
½   **Tablespoon chile oil**
¼   cup olive oil

1   Tablespoon minced garlic
1   cup dry sherry
¾   cup minced red onion
½   teaspoon black pepper
½   teaspoon white pepper
¼   cup plus 2 Tablespoons
    balsamic vinegar
    juice of one lemon
    juice of one lime

Blend all ingredients in a food processor for five minutes. Keep refrigerated and it will last about 1 month.

Yield: About 1-¼ cups
Heat Scale: Extremely Hot

wwwwwwwww

JALAPEÑO-MINT DIJON MUSTARD
Sim's Catering, Washington, New Jersey

Sim's Catering is a combination specialty food store, a deli-restaurant, and an off-premise caterer. Owners Sim and Angie Baron left their respective careers as electrical engineer and mortgage banker to prepare spicy cuisines from many countries. Sim says that this mustard is wonderful with fish, cheese, or sandwiches.

2 cups dry white wine	2 teaspoons salt
1 large Spanish onion, chopped	**2 Tablespoons minced**
4 cloves garlic, mashed	**pickled jalapeños**
1 cup dry mustard powder	2 Tablespoons fresh mint leaves
3 Tablespoons honey	(or 1 Tablespoon dried),
1 Tablespoon vegetable oil	chopped

In a nonreactive saucepan, combine the wine, onions, and garlic. Heat to boiling, reduce heat, and simmer for 5 minutes. Strain and discard solids. Return the liquid to the pan, add the dry mustard, honey, oil, and salt. On low heat, stir constantly until thick. Add the jalapeños and mint leaves and cool.

Place in a covered 1 pint jar and age in a cool, dry place for 2 to 8 weeks. Refrigerate after aging.

Yield: 1-½ cups
Heat Scale: Medium

SPICY BANANA SAUCE
Miss Pearl's Jam House, San Francisco, California

Chef Joey Altman describes his restaurant thusly: "While the decor appears to be salvaged from a pirate ship and is somewhat whimsical, the cuisine is as serious as the drinks are potent." He says that this sauce was developed to accompany grilled sea bass, but it can be served with any other grilled fish.

1	**pasilla chile,** stem removed, seeded	½	cup lime juice
½	**teaspoon cayenne powder**	3	cloves garlic
2	medium-ripe bananas	1	inch peeled and sliced ginger
1	bunch green onions, green part only	1-½	cups olive oil
			salt and pepper to taste

Place all ingredients in a blender except the oil, salt, and pepper. Blend on high until a smooth consistency is reached. You might have to use a rubber spatula to remove the sauce off the sides of the blender. While it is pureeing, drizzle in the oil until it is all emulsified. Season with salt and pepper and serve at room temperature.

Yield: 2 cups
Heat Scale: Medium

〜〜〜〜〜〜〜〜〜〜

CALYPSO JERK RUB
Calypso Caribbean Cuisine, Houston, Texas

Calypso owner and chef Tim McGann is a former Caribbean beer importer and a reggae music promoter who started collecting recipes from the islands and finally opened his own restaurant. He believes that because of the blending of island spices with native herbs, fruits, and vegetables, the Caribbean "has one of the most innovative cuisines on earth."

Here is his version of the classic Jamaican marinade and basting sauce for chicken, pork, fish, or shrimp.

2 to 5 Scotch bonnet
(Habanero) chiles, stems
removed
30 black peppercorns, freshly
ground (1 teaspoon ground)
15 allspice berries, freshly
ground (1 Tablespoon
ground)
1 cup chopped white onion
1 cup chopped scallions, white
part only

4 Tablespoons fresh thyme
2 Tablespoons Worcestershire
sauce
2 Tablespoons bottled liquid
smoke (optional)
4 Tablespoons vegetable oil
1 Tablespoon minced garlic
1 Tablespoon ground cinnamon
½ cup green onion tops

Combine all ingredients except the green onion tops in a food processor or blender and make a paste. In a saucepan, combine the paste and the green onion tops and heat until the onions wilt. Remove from the heat and refrigerate for use as a marinade and basting sauce.

Yield: 1-½ cups
Heat Scale: Hot to Extremely Hot

〰〰〰〰〰〰〰

TRINIDAD PEPPER RELISH
Pier House Restaurant, Key West, Florida

The inhabitants of this southernmost city in the continental United States are so independent that they refer to their island as "The Conch Republic." One of the dining landmarks there is the Pier House, which has the enviable address of Number One Duval Street, in the heart of the tourist area. The recipe below, from executive chef Brent Holleman, is indicative of the population's taste for the hot and spicy. This sauce, reminiscent of Matouk's bottled hot sauce, is served over their Eleutheran Burger but can also be used as a relish for seafood and grilled meats.

15 **Scotch bonnet (Habanero) peppers,** stems removed, seeded, and minced
 2 large white onions, minced
 1 papaya, peeled and diced
 1 mango, peeled, pitted, and diced

 2 Tablespoons Dijon mustard
½ teaspoon turmeric
½ teaspoon curry powder
 3 cups vinegar

Place all ingredients in a pan, bring to a boil, lower the heat, and simmer for thirty minutes. Remove from the heat, cool, and store the sauce in a jar in the refrigerator.

Yield: 1-½ to 2 quarts
Heat Scale: Extremely Hot

〰〰〰〰〰〰〰

SANTA FE GREEN CHILE SAUCE
Outlaws Steakhouse and Cantina, Orlando, Florida

Restaurateur Bill Hattaway, former president of General Mills Restaurants, has opened literally hundreds of restaurants all over the country—mostly Red Lobsters and Olive Gardens. He gave up that source of fame and fortune to become an independent, and Outlaws is his first project. To ensure authenticity, he retained Bill Weiland, president of the American Culinary Federation Chefs of Santa Fe, to assist in the development of recipes such as this one, which can be served as a soup or as an enchilada sauce.

½ cup finely diced onions
 1 Tablespoon minced garlic
 3 Tablespoons vegetable oil
 1 Tablespoon flour
 1 cup chicken stock

1-½ **cups diced New Mexican green chile** that has been stemmed, roasted, peeled, and seeded
 1 cup chopped tomatoes
 1 Tablespoon minced cilantro

Sauté the onion and garlic in the oil until soft. Whisk in the flour, stirring constantly. Add the stock and continue to whisk until thickened. Add the remaining ingredients and cook for 10 minutes.

Yield: 2 cups
Heat Scale: Medium

~~~~~~~~~~~~~~~~~~~~

EL CHOLO GREEN CHILE SAUCE
El Cholo Mexican Restaurant, Los Angeles, California

In 1927, George and Aurelia Salisbury opened El Cholo in a small store-front across the street from its present location. Ron Salisbury, a third-generation restaurateur, now runs the operation plus three additional restaurants. This recipe is the creation of chef Roberto Juárez. It can be served over grilled poultry or fish.

8	**New Mexican green chiles,** roasted, peeled, seeded, and stems removed	1	teaspoon oregano
		2	cloves garlic, minced
		½	to ¾ cup sour cream
1-½	cups chicken broth		

Simmer the chiles, oregano, and garlic in the chicken broth until the broth is reduced by one-half (about 20 minutes).

Just before serving, stir in the sour cream to taste, consistency, and heat, remembering that the more sour cream, the less spiciness.

Yield: 1-¼ cups
Heat Scale: Medium

FRESH TART CHERRY AND ANCHO CHILE CHUTNEY

Rudy V's Restaurant, Eastgate Holiday Inn, Cincinnati, Ohio

Executive chef Cheryl Schatzman of Rudy V's says that she is educating the diners of Cincinnati about the many varieties of chiles she uses in her elegant steakhouse. To lure them into the chile cult, she serves this innovative chutney with grilled veal chops.

2 **ancho chiles,** stems removed, seeded, and coarsely chopped

1 **jalapeño chile,** stem removed, seeded, and minced

4 pounds fresh tart cherries, pitted

1 yellow bell pepper, seeded and coarsely chopped

1 red bell pepper, seeded and coarsely chopped

2 cloves garlic, minced

¼ cup golden raisins

½ cup cider vinegar

1 cup molasses

¼ cup honey

1 piece star anise

1 teaspoon freshly grated cinnamon

1 teaspoon freshly grated nutmeg

Combine all ingredients in a nonreactive pot. Cook uncovered over medium heat for 45 minutes. Remove the star anise after 20 minutes so its taste does not dominate.

Yield: 6 cups
Heat Scale: Mild

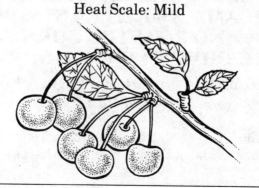

THAI BEEF SALAD
Claire Restaurant, New York, New York

The original Claire opened in Key West in 1978 and the New York Claire premiered in 1982. It is a colorful, tropical restaurant with overhead fans and an island decor. The owner, Marvin Paige, works closely with chef Dhanit Choladda to create a very hands-on operation in both concept and menu. They call this salad creation "bracing, tangy, and addictive."

2 pounds ground beef	2 Tablespoons diced red onion
1 Tablespoon minced garlic	½ **teaspoon hot crushed red chile**
2 Tablespoons fish sauce	1 Tablespoon chopped cilantro
¼ cup freshly squeezed lime juice	romaine leaves

In a skillet, sauté the ground beef, fish sauce, lime juice, and garlic (use no oil) until nearly dry. Remove from heat and drain off any excess grease. Add the onions, crushed chile, and cilantro and stir until well mixed.

     To serve, roll the mixture into the romaine leaves.

Serves: 6

Heat Scale: Mild

〰〰〰〰〰〰〰

GRILLED CHICKEN SALAD WITH JICAMA, TORTILLA STRIPS, AND ROASTED CORN WITH CHIPOTLE VINAIGRETTE
La Tour Restaurant, Park Hyatt Hotel, Chicago, Illinois

Executive chef Charles Weber, who came to La Tour from The Mark in West Palm Beach, Florida, is a fan of both fresh herbs and chile peppers.

He says, "One way of introducing their flavors indirectly to dishes is by the use of flavored vinegars, oils, and even honey." This rather complicated (but worthwhile) recipe is a good example of his philosophy, but first it is necessary to construct the Chipotle-Thyme Vinegar and the Annato-Habanero Oil. Although technically a salad, this dish can also be served as an entree.

CHIPOTLE-THYME VINEGAR

2 quarts balsamic vinegar
2 cups chipotle chiles

¼ cup bruised thyme leaves

Bring the vinegar to a boil in a nonreactive pan, pour it over the chiles and thyme, let cool, cover, and let it steep for one week. Shake the container once a day.

ANNATO-HABANERO OIL

½ cup annato seeds
1 quart grapeseed oil

2 to 4 Habanero chiles scored on the bottom (you select the heat)

Place the annato seeds in a jar. Heat the oil to 180 degrees, pour it over the seeds, and then add the chiles. Let sit for one week.

THE MARINADE

1 jalapeño, stem removed, seeded, and minced
1 cup olive oil

2 cloves garlic, minced
⅛ cup cilantro, minced

Mix all ingredients together.

CHIPOTLE VINAIGRETTE

½ cup Chipotle-Thyme Vinegar
2 shallots, minced
2 cloves garlic, minced

½ cup avocado oil
¼ cup Annato-Habanero Oil
1 teaspoon minced cilantro

Whisk together all ingredients in a bowl.

THE SALAD

3 whole chicken breasts, split
   kernels of 2 roasted cobs of corn
   The Marinade
1 small jicama, peeled and
   julienned
1 red bell pepper, seeded and
   julienned
1 small red onion, julienned

2 heads Boston lettuce, washed
   and cut up
1 bunch watercress, washed and
   trimmed
3 corn tortillas cut into strips
   and fried in corn oil until
   crisp
   Chipotle Vinaigrette

Marinate the chicken breasts in the marinade overnight. Grill the chicken breasts until done, and at the same time grill the two cobs of corn and remove the kernels. Remove the chicken from the bones and chop coarsely.

Combine all ingredients and toss with the Chipotle Vinaigrette.

Serves: 6
Heat Scale: Medium

wwwwwwwwwww

GRILLED PORK LOIN SALAD WITH SUN-DRIED TOMATO VINAIGRETTE
Maple Leaf Grill, Seattle, Washington

Owners Rip Ripley and David Albert refer to the Maple Leaf as a great neighborhood "joint" where patrons can either stop by for a Northwest micro-brew on tap and watch a ballgame on TV, or hang around and become a serious "foodist" by sampling one of Rip's nightly specials. This salad, which can also be served as an entree, features a unique dry rub for the pork.

ANCHO CHILE DRY RUB

4	**ancho chiles,** stems removed and seeded	1	teaspoon thyme
2	teaspoons whole white peppercorns	1	small bay leaf
1	teaspoon whole black peppercorns	1	teaspoon annato seeds
½	teaspoon celery seed	1-½	teaspoons salt
3-½	teaspoons cumin seed		olive oil
			3-pound boneless pork loin

Grind or blend together all the ingredients except the olive oil and pork loin. Mix the rub with the olive oil in the proportion of 1 tablespoon dry rub to 1 teaspoon oil. Rub the mixture over the pork loin and marinate in the refrigerator overnight.

SUN-DRIED TOMATO VINAIGRETTE

12	sun-dried tomatoes, chopped	¼	teaspoon salt
2	Tablespoons parsley	½	cup white wine vinegar
1-½	Tablespoons chopped cilantro	⅛	cup balsamic vinegar
5	to 6 scallions, chopped	1-¼	cup olive oil
½	teaspoon pepper		

Combine all ingredients and mix well. Allow to sit for an hour to mix the flavors.

THE SALAD

the marinated pork loin	1 jicama, peeled and julienned
Sun-dried Tomato Vinaigrette	2 cucumbers, peeled and julienned
mixed greens such as spinach, mustard greens, or argula	quartered tomatoes for garnish

Slice the pork loin into ¼-inch thick slices and grill until done. Toss the vinaigrette with the greens, jicama, and cucumber and place in salad bowls. Place the grilled pork slices over the greens. Garnish with quartered tomatoes.

Serves: 6
Heat Scale: Mild

~~~~~~~~~~~~~~~~~~~

CHICKEN TACO SALAD
Quaker Steak & Lube, Sharon, Pennsylvania

Many restaurants throughout the country are serving innovative salads that combine vegetables, meats, and dressings made with a variety of hot sauces. At the Quaker Steak, a remodeled gas station filled with automotive memorabilia, they serve this salad, which lives up to their philosophy that "spice is nice."

THE DRESSING
3 **Tablespoons of your favorite bottled hot sauce**
¼ cup mayonnaise

½ cup prepared guacamole (see recipe, page 145)

Combine all ingredients, mix well, and refrigerate.

THE SALAD
1 pound boned, skinned chicken breasts, cut into small cubes
2 Tablespoons cooking oil
¼ cup minced onions
¼ cup minced bell peppers
¼ **cup of your favorite salsa** (see recipes this chapter)
1 4-ounce can pimientos, chopped

10 lettuce leaves
5 cups tostada chips
5 cups shredded lettuce
2 cups cooked kidney beans
½ cup chopped tomatoes
The Dressing
1 cup shredded cheddar cheese

Sauté the chicken in the cooking oil for 2 minutes. Add the onions and bell peppers and sauté 1 minute more. Add the salsa and pimiento and simmer 5 minutes. Reserve and keep warm.

Line 5 bowls with leaf lettuce. Arrange tostada chips on the lettuce artistically. Place the shredded lettuce within the chips. Top the lettuce with the kidney beans and then the chicken mixture. Sprinkle on the tomato, add the dressing, and top with the cheddar cheese.

Serves: 5
Heat Scale: Mild

∿∿∿∿∿∿∿∿∿∿∿

ENSALADA DE NOPALES
Fonda San Miguel, Austin, Texas

Miguel Ravago, chef and co-owner of this gorgeous, hacienda-style restaurant, has trained with such renowned chefs as Diana Kennedy and Patricia Quintana. He serves interior and coastal Mexican cuisines accompanied by a wide range of sauces. This salad calls for *nopales,* the leaves of the prickly pear cactus. They are available fresh in some markets and elsewhere canned.

2 Tablespoons olive oil
1 pound (3-½ cups) nopales (cactus pads), cleaned and diced
1 clove garlic, chopped
2 heaping Tablespoons chopped white onion
½ teaspoon sea salt
2 **serrano chiles,** stems removed, chopped

1 teaspoon dried oregano
¼ cup tequila
   garnish: chopped cilantro, chopped red onion, sliced avocados, sliced tomatoes, and crumbled feta cheese
corn tortillas

Heat the oil in a heavy frying pan and add the nopales, garlic, white onion, and salt. Cover the pan and cook over low heat until the nopales are tender, about 5 minutes. Add the chiles, oregano, and tequila and stir. Remove from heat, drain, and cool.

Place the cactus mixture on 4 plates. Add the garnishes in the order listed and serve the salad with fresh corn tortillas.

Serves: 4
Heat Scale: Mild

~~~~~~~~~~~~~~~~

WARM LOBSTER SALAD WITH A CHIPOTLE VINAIGRETTE
Miss Pearl's Jam House, San Francisco, California

Miss Pearl's spicy and innovative menu, by chef Joey Altman, offers such treats as Eggs over Evil for breakfast, 7-Chile Bar-B-Q Pork Sandwich for lunch, and Angry Pork (He's Back and Madder Than Ever) for dinner. This salad features a Miss Pearl trademark: the combination of hot chiles, seafood, fruit, and fresh herbs.

THE VINAIGRETTE

3 **chipotle chiles,** lightly toasted, stem and seeds removed
½ cup orange juice
¾ cup lime juice
1-½ cups olive oil

1 teaspoon honey
2 shallots, minced
4 cloves garlic, minced
⅛ teaspoon ground cumin, toasted
salt and pepper to taste

In a blender, place the chiles, ¼ cup of the orange juice, ½ cup of the lime juice, and puree. Drizzle in 1 cup of oil while this mixture purees. Pour this mixture into a bowl and whisk in the honey, shallots, garlic, cumin, and the remaining orange juice, lime juice, and oil. Season with salt and pepper if desired.

THE SALAD

4 large handfuls mixed baby lettuce leaves

2 avocados, pitted and sliced

2 oranges, peeled, cleaned, separated into sections, and seeds removed

meat of 2 boiled lobsters (1-½ pounds each), shredded and kept warm

The Vinaigrette

1 bunch cilantro, leaves picked

On individual salad plates, dress the greens. Arrange the avocado slices, orange slices, and shredded lobster meat artistically on the plates. Drizzle the vinaigrette over the salad and garnish with the cilantro leaves.

Serves: 4

Heat Scale: Medium

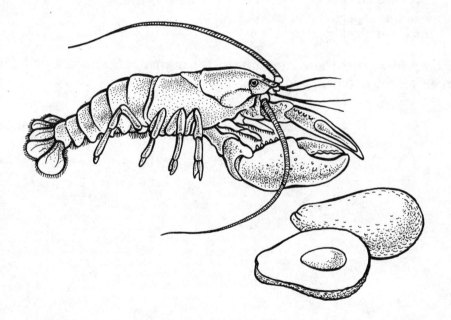

EQUATORIAL FRUIT SALAD WITH LIME JUICE AND JALAPEÑOS

East Coast Grill, Cambridge, Massachusetts

Chef Chris Schlesinger confesses he's been addicted to chiles since he discovered them in Barbados over ten years ago. "It's challenging cooking with them," he says. "And the nice thing is they are inexpensive. They are the ingredients of the people. They aren't heavy. People will never have to worry about getting gout. This is a clean, healthy cuisine." Chris is the author of *The Thrill of the Grill* (Morrow, 1990).

3   **red jalapeños,** stems removed, seeded, and minced

1   ripe mango, pitted and cut into ½-inch cubes

1   ripe banana, peeled and cut into ½-inch cubes

1   ripe papaya, peeled, seeded, and cut into ½-inch cubes

½   pineapple, peeled, cored, and cut into ½-inch cubes

   juice of 3 limes

In a large, decorative bowl, combine all the ingredients and mix well. For a true Caribbean touch, add a splash of rum.

Serves: 6
Heat Scale: Medium

Spectacular Soups and Stews

Because early cultures lacked the cooking tools we take for granted, the earliest cooked recipes tended to be simple. Undoubtedly, the first cooking implement was a sharpened stick for holding pieces of meat over a fire, but second to that was the cooking pot. Thus it is logical to assume that the first combination dishes were soups and stews made in the days before farming and domesticated animals. Wild vegetables such as turnips, onions, and radishes were boiled with game to make the earliest soups and stews.

Despite the simplicity of technique involved in heating liquids in a pot over a flame, today's soups and stews are far from simple. Some utilize multiple cooking techniques such as broiling a cheese-topped stew or adding fried ingredients to a soup. Some involve the manipulation of over twenty ingredients, which can be quite time-consuming but well worth the effort.

One particular version of stew has captivated the imagination of cooks and chefs all over the United States. That, of course, is chili con carne. There are at least four hundred chili cookoffs each year in this country and a seemingly infinite number of variations on the same dish. Every chili cook—and most hate being called "chef"—sincerely believes that his chili is the best in the world. In this chapter, we're going to have our own chili cookoff. Fiery food experts have provided five different recipes: it's up to home cooks to determine the winner.

CHILE-CORN CHOWDER
The Pink Adobe, Santa Fe, New Mexico

Rosalea Murphy, the living legend of Santa Fe restaurants, serves a unique blend of cuisines, including Southern, Anglo-American, Hispanic, and Native American. She is the author of two cookbooks, including the splendid *Pink Adobe Cookbook* (Dell, 1988). This hearty chowder is great on cold winter days and should be served with heated rolled flour tortillas or corn muffins.

3	corn tortillas, cut into thin strips	3-½	cups chicken broth
1	cup cooking oil for frying	¾	cup half-and-half plus ¼ cup whipping cream
½	cup butter	1	cup grated cheddar cheese
2	cups sliced fresh mushrooms	2-½	cups cooked whole kernel corn
1	onion, choppped		
1	**small jalapeño,** stem and seeds removed, chopped	¼	cup drained and chopped pimiento
½	**cup chopped New Mexican green chile**		salt to taste
1	teaspoon cumin seed	4	cups parsley or cilantro, chopped (for garnish)
½	cup flour		
½	**teaspoon ground red chile powder**		

First, prepare the tortilla strips. Heat the oil in a 10-inch skillet until hot and then cook the tortilla strips in batches until crisp, about 1 minute. Drain on paper towels and set aside.

In a soup kettle, heat 2 tablespoons of the butter and cook the mushrooms until brown. Remove and set aside.

Add the remaining butter to the kettle and cook the onion, jalapeño, green chile, and cumin seed until the onion is soft. Add the flour and chile powder and cook, stirring constantly, for 3 minutes to make a roux. Stir in the broth and half-and-half with the whipping cream. Cook the mixture, stirring constantly, until it is smooth and thick. Add the reserved mushrooms, half of the cheese, the corn, and the pimiento, and salt to taste. Cook and stir for 2 or 3 minutes.

Break the tortilla strips into six heated soup bowls. Sprinkle the remaining cheese over the strips, and then ladle the soup into the bowls. Garnish with the chopped parsley or cilantro.

Serves: 6
Heat Scale: Medium

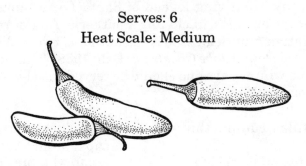

NEW ORLEANS RED BEAN SOUP
On the Verandah, Highlands, North Carolina

Alan and Marta Figel, who opened On the Verandah in 1981, have an avid interest in hot and spicy foods, as indicated by their hot sauce collection, which now numbers nearly five hundred bottles from all over the world. Their menu features spicy foods from everywhere as well. Alan's Cajun soup, below, is one of his customers' favorites.

4	quarts water	2	cups celery, minced
1	pound red or kidney beans	6	large bay leaves
½	**cup serrano chiles,** stems removed, seeded, and minced	1	Tablespoon salt
		2	Tablespoons freshly ground pepper
1	pound smoked ham hock	1	Tablespoon dried thyme leaf
2	cups onion, minced		

Bring the water to a boil, add the beans, and boil for 2 minutes. Turn off the heat and let the beans soak for 2 hours.

Strain off the liquid to measure and return it to the pot, adding enough water to make 4 quarts. Add the remaining ingredients and simmer at least 4 hours, adding back water to keep the liquid at 4 quarts.

Puree half the beans and vegetables in a blender and return them to the soup. The ham hock may be served separately or diced and returned to the pot.

Yield: 4 quarts
Heat Scale: Medium

∿∿∿∿∿∿∿∿∿∿∿∿

COMPADRES TORTILLA SOUP WITH SALSA FRESCA
Compadres Mexican Bar and Grill, Honolulu, Hawaii

A great Mexican restaurant in Hawaii? Yes, indeed, and there's even a Compadres in Brisbane, Australia. The Honolulu Compadres has been named one of the twenty best restaurants in Hawaii, and it sponsors a highly successful chili con carne cookoff in August. Executive Chef Alfonso Navarro, a native of Jalisco, Mexico, oversees the menu, which offers a wide variety of Mexican specialties, including this tasty soup.

SALSA FRESCA

2 **serrano chiles** (or more to taste), stems removed, seeded, and chopped

2 large tomatoes, peeled, seeded, and diced

6 green onions, chopped, including the tops

1 avocado, peeled, pitted, and diced

fresh cilantro to taste, chopped

juice of ½ lime

salt to taste

Combine all ingredients in a bowl and mix with a wooden spoon. Allow to sit for at least an hour to blend the flavors.

Yield: 1-½ cups
Heat Scale: Mild to Medium

TORTILLA SOUP

1 large chicken
½ onion, chopped
2 stalks celery, chopped
1 bay leaf
1 teaspoon black peppercorns
3 corn tortillas, cut into strips

vegetable oil for deep frying
2 cups grated provolone or mozzarella cheese
chopped cilantro for garnish
Salsa Fresca

Place the first five ingredients in a large stockpot, cover with water, and bring to a boil. Reduce heat and simmer for about an hour until the chicken is cooked. Allow the chicken to cool in the liquid, then remove it to a platter. Skin and bone the chicken and shred the meat. Strain the broth through cheesecloth and reserve.

Fry the tortilla strips in oil until crisp. For each serving, place ½ cup of shredded chicken in an ovenproof soup bowl. Pour in the chicken stock, add the tortilla strips, and sprinkle with the cheese. Place the bowls under the broiler until the cheese melts. Sprinkle with the cilantro and top with Salsa Fresca to taste.

Serves: 6
Heat Scale: Mild

JALAPEÑO COLBY CHEESE SOUP

Rudy V's Restaurant, Eastgate Holiday Inn, Cincinnati, Ohio

The sentiment behind the fiery food cooked up by Cheryl Schatzman, executive chef at Rudy V's, is telling: "Foods with spice and bite manifest themselves on the palate as *wow!*" This thick and hearty soup, which gets its bite from jalapeño cheese, is a perfect lunch dish served during a snowy and cold winter afternoon of football.

¼ cup butter
1 small onion, minced
1 small bunch celery hearts, minced
½ cup flour
2 quarts chicken stock

1 pound jalapeño cheese, shredded
½ pound Colby cheese, shredded
2 cups heavy cream
1 small bunch celery hearts, minced, for garnish

Melt the butter in a large soup pot and sauté the onions and celery until transparent. Add the flour, stir, and blend for about 30 seconds. Add the chicken stock, turn the heat to medium-high, and stir with a whisk. Add the cheeses, reduce heat to medium, and continue to whisk for 5 minutes.

Add the cream, reduce heat to low, and cook for 10 minutes, continuing to whisk so the soup will not scorch.

Serve garnished with the celery hearts.

Serves: 8 to 10
Heat Scale: Mild to Medium

~~~~~~~~~~~~~~~~~~

CREAM OF POBLANO SOUP

El Cholo Mexican Restaurant, Los Angeles, California

Roberto Juárez, the chef of El Cholo for over ten years, likes to blend the sweet with the spicy, and this recipe certainly manifests that technique. This soup tends to be mild, so to spice it up, add small amounts of the hottest chile powder in your spice cabinet.

3 poblano chiles, roasted, peeled, seeds and stems removed, chopped
½ cup diced onion
¼ cup diced carrot
2 Tablespoons clarified butter
2 Tablespoons flour

4 cups chicken stock
1 Tablespoon chopped fresh cilantro
¾ cup whipping cream
   salt to taste
8 tostada chips
4 slices Monterey Jack cheese

Sauté the chiles, onions, and carrot in the butter for about 5 minutes, then stir in the flour and cook over low heat for an additional 5 minutes. Whisk in the chicken stock and simmer for 30 minutes.

Remove this mixture from the heat and puree in a blender. Return it to a soup pot and continue to simmer. Add the cilantro and cream and season to taste with salt.

Ladle the soup into 4 heat-proof cups and top each with 2 tostada chips and 1 slice of cheese. Place under the broiler until the cheese melts.

Serves: 4
Heat Scale: Mild

ᐧᐧᐧᐧᐧᐧᐧᐧᐧᐧᐧᐧᐧ

SPICY STONE CRAB
GAZPACHO WITH BASIL
Pier House Restaurant, Key West, Florida

The philosophy of the Pier House maintains that "there should be a balance of the different spices and chiles with the main ingredients that they complement." This simple yet interesting soup, a creation of executive chef Brent Holleman, certainly upholds that idea by blending together fresh vegetables—including some jalapeños.

3 jalapeños, stems removed, seeded, and coarsely chopped

½ **cup hot sauce such as Tabasco**

15 tomatoes, peeled

5 bell peppers, stems removed, seeded

2 large yellow onions, peeled and coarsely chopped

6 cucumbers, peeled, seeded, and coarsely chopped

1 bunch fresh cilantro

2 bunches fresh basil

1 Tablespoon freshly ground pepper

1 quart V-8 Juice
salt to taste

8 stone crab claws which have been steamed or boiled

Place all ingredients except crab claws in a blender and blend until semi-smooth, leaving some chunks in. Cooks with a small blender may have to do this in small batches. Add some salt to taste, chill the mixture, and serve garnished with a stone crab claw, or substitute a lobster claw.

Serves: 8
Heat Scale: Hot

THAI COCONUT-CHICKEN SOUP
Restaurant Muse, Hermosa Beach, California

With a clientele described as "a mixture of movers and shakers making a difference in Los Angeles and the world," the food at Restaurant Muse better be top-notch. Owner Ron Braun and chef Vaughn Allen believe in a healthy and clean approach to dining that highlights the hot and spicy. The chiles used in their recipes include chipotle, New Mexican, jalapeño, ancho, and Thai.

3   cups chicken stock
1   chicken breast and 1 thigh, boned, skinned, and cut into bite-sized pieces
1/3 cup sliced and peeled ginger root
1   stalk lemon grass, cut into 8 pieces
2   cans coconut milk

1   **Tablespoon hot Thai chile paste** (or substitute other chile paste; see page 7)
1   **Tablespoon fish sauce**
1   can straw mushrooms
1   Tablespoon lemon juice
    cilantro sprigs for garnish

Combine the stock, chicken, and ginger in a saucepan and bring to a boil. Add the lemon grass, reduce heat, and simmer for 5 minutes. Add the coconut milk, the chile paste, fish sauce, and mushrooms and simmer for another 5 minutes. Add the lemon juice and simmer for yet another 5 minutes.

Remove the larger pieces of lemon grass and ginger, garnish with the cilantro, and serve.

Serves: 4 to 6
Heat Scale: Medium

wwwwwwwwwwwwww

SAN PASQUAL'S RED PEPPER SOUP
Pasqual's Southwestern Deli, Madison, Wisconsin

As evidence that hot and spicy foods have infiltrated the northern land of cheese, beer, and bratwurst, we present Pasqual's, a Santa Fe-styled deli named after the patron saint of the kitchen, San Pasqual. Owner Tim Guilfoil notes that his restaurant (which also has another location in Minneapolis), "re-creates the unique atmosphere of the Southwest." Pasqual's is also innovative, as this soup demonstrates.

6   large red bell peppers, roasted, peeled, seeded, and cut into quarters
1   **jalapeño,** stem removed, seeded and minced (or more for heat)
1   onion, diced
1   clove garlic, minced
3   Tablespoons olive oil
5   cups freshly made chicken stock
1   **Tablespoon adobo sauce** from chipotles in adobo sauce
½   teaspoon cumin
1   teaspoon basil
1   teaspoon oregano
    sour cream for garnish
    minced green onion for garnish

Puree the red bell peppers in a food processor.

Sauté the jalapeño, onion, and garlic in the olive oil until soft, about 5 minutes. Add the red bell puree, chicken broth, adobo sauce, and spices and simmer 30 minutes. The soup can be thickened with cornstarch if necessary.

After the soup has been ladled into serving bowls, swirl in a dollop of sour cream and sprinkle with the green onions.

Serves: 4
Heat Scale: Mild to Medium

wwwwwwwww

PECOS RIVER RED XX CHILI
The Loon Café, Minneapolis, Minnesota

Jeff Johnson, manager of The Loon, says that because of the extremely cold winters in Minneapolis, chili and other hot and spicy foods have developed "quite a religious following." The restaurant has been open for over ten years and specializes in five different kinds of chilis, which year after year win readers' polls in various magazines and newspapers. The recipe for the number-one selling chili at The Loon is given below, in a quantity large enough to serve at a party.

5 pounds trimmed beef (no fat), cut into small cubes
1 large onion, chopped fine
1 **cup chopped New Mexican green chile**
⅓ **cup cayenne powder**
½ **cup New Mexican red chile powder**
1 **cup paprika**
2 **Tablespoons minced jalapeños**
2 **Tablespoons crushed red chile**

2 Tablespoons cumin
1 Tablespoon oregano
2 quarts tomato sauce
2 cups water
1 **dash Tabasco Sauce**
3 Tablespoons chicken base
1 cup masa harina (corn flour)
2 cups water
salt to taste
cheddar cheese, minced green onions, and sour cream for garnish

In a large pot, brown together the beef, onion, and green chile. Add the cayenne, chile powder, paprika, jalapeños, crushed red chile, cumin, and oregano. Simmer for 15 minutes.

Add the tomato sauce, water, Tabasco, and chicken base and simmer for 20 minutes.

Mix the masa harina with the water and make an extremely smooth paste. Add this to the pot, stirring constantly. Simmer for 15 minutes, or until the meat is tender. Add salt to taste if necessary.

Serve the chili topped with shredded cheddar cheese, minced green onions, and a dollop of sour cream.

Serves: 10 or more

Heat Scale: Hot

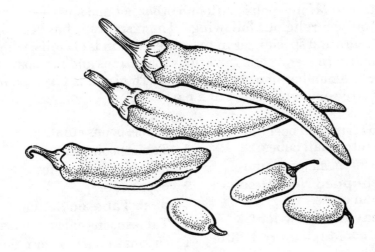

ED'S BUFFALO SNORT RED CHILI
Texas Chili and Rib Company, Phoenix, Arizona

Ed Dorfman, winner of many awards and trophies for his barbecue and chili, says that the ambience of his restaurant is that of a small Texas bar. Basically a carry-out, his "small joint" seats about thirty people who dig into his brisket, ribs, chicken wings, and several different kinds of chili. About his love for chiles, he calls himself a "capsaicin-holic" who uses chile in everything he cooks—note the eight chile-laden ingredients of this recipe.

½ pound bacon with fat

2 pounds Spanish onions, chopped fine

5 **Tablespoons New Mexican red chile powder**

2 **Tablespoons cayenne powder**

4 **jalapeño chiles,** stems removed, seeded, and chopped

½ **cup canned New Mexican green chiles,** chopped

1 **dried red New Mexican chile pod,** stem removed

1 **pound Italian hot sausage**

dash Tabasco hot sauce

1 **teaspoon Hungarian hot paprika**

3 pounds crushed Italian tomatoes

1 Tablespoon Mexican oregano

10 ounces T-bone steak, chopped fine

5 pounds coarsely ground chuck

1-½ cups water

1 bottle Lone Star Beer

2 teaspoons salt

1-½ cups chopped bell pepper

1 Tablespoon garlic in oil, chopped

2 Tablespoons Worcestershire sauce

1 Tablespoon raw sugar

5 Tablespoons cumin

1 pound fresh armadillo meat (optional)

Fry the bacon in a soup kettle, add the onion, and sauté until soft. Add the remaining ingredients and bring to a boil. Reduce heat and simmer for about two hours, stirring frequently.

Serves: 8 to 10

Heat Scale: Hot

ED'S BUFFALO SNORT GREEN CHILI
Texas Chili and Rib Company, Phoenix, Arizona

He's been called a "chili doctor," a "barbecue baron," a "chili guru," and a "spiceologist," but he says that he's just a chef who, through trial and error, has invented recipes that people other than himself enjoy. Despite all his awards, he believes that the best chili judges are his customers.

3	Tablespoons bacon fat	**2**	**teaspoons Tabasco sauce**
1	cup chopped scallions	12	small tomatillos, quartered
2	teaspoons crushed garlic	2	Tablespoons Mexican oregano
3	pounds pork loin, cut into ¼-inch cubes	3	Tablespoons cumin
2	**cups canned New Mexican green chiles,** chopped	2	teaspoons salt
		1-½	Tablespoons dried cilantro
6	**NuMex Big Jim green chiles,** stems removed, roasted, peeled, seeded, and chopped	1	Tablespoon brown sugar
		4	chicken bouillon cubes
		1	bottle beer
4	**jalapeños,** stems removed, seeded, and chopped	1	Tablespoon filé powder

Sauté the scallions and garlic in the bacon fat until soft. Add the pork loin and sear until crisp. Add the rest of the ingredients and simmer until done, approximately two hours.

Serves: 6 to 8
Heat Scale: Medium to Hot

MARIA'S CHILI VERDE
Maria's of Keno, Klamath Falls, Oregon

"I am probably the world's finest cooker of chili," states Bud Spillar, owner/chef of Maria's of Keno, a claim that will undoubtedly be disputed by all the other chefs represented in this book. In support of his declaration, Bud has won chili cookoffs in El Paso and Austin, placed fourth in the Great Northwest Chili Cookoff, and is frequently a judge at the famous Terlingua cookoff in Texas. Home cooks can judge for themselves by fixing this hot and colorful concoction.

2	pounds skirt or flank steak	1	teaspoon salt
3	quarts beef bouillon	4	Tablespoons Mexican oregano
12	**fresh jalapeños,** stems removed, diced with seeds	1	large onion, diced
3-½	**cups canned chopped New Mexican chiles**	1	Tablespoon granulated garlic
1	**Habanero chile,** stem removed, seeded, and diced (optional)	12	strips Monterey Jack cheese cut ½-inch by 2 inches

Cook the steak in a pressure cooker with 2 cups of water at 10 pounds pressure for 1 hour. Remove the steak, shred, and keep warm.

Place the bouillon in a stock pot, add the remaining ingredients except the cheese, and bring to a boil. Reduce heat and simmer for 30 minutes.

Place the broth mixture in bowls, add the shredded steak, and add 2 pieces of cheese to form a cross in the bowl. Serve with corn or flour tortillas brushed with butter.

Serves: 6 to 8
Heat Scale: Hot to Extremely Hot

BLACK BEAN CHILI
Galley del Mar, Ridgeland, Mississippi

The Galley del Mar is an "upscale resort-area restaurant for fine, casual dining," according to owners Wayne Craft and Larry McCandless. Its specialty is spicy seafood dishes prepared by a collaboration of their cooking staff supervised by Lloyd Kent, but occasionally they veer off into the area of chili con carne. This is one of the more unusual chili recipes submitted to *Hot Spots*.

1 pound black beans, cleaned
1 **Tablespoon red chile powder**
1 Tablespoon cumin
2 teaspoons paprika
1 Tablespoon oregano
1 bay leaf
1 Tablespoon olive oil
1 onion, chopped
4 cloves garlic, minced
1 bell pepper, seeded and chopped
2 cups canned chopped Rotel tomatoes with liquid
2 **jalapeños,** stems removed, seeded, and chopped (or more for heat)

1 **dried red New Mexican chile,** stem and seeds removed
½ **teaspoon cayenne powder**
1 Tablespoon chopped fresh cilantro
1 pound tenderloin tips, cubed
2 teaspoons salt
1-½ teaspoons black pepper
1 ham hock
3 cups canned peeled tomatoes with liquid
½ cup Burgundy wine
fresh cilantro for garnish

Soak the beans overnight in water. Drain and refill the pot until the water just covers the beans, and bring to a boil. Reduce heat and simmer 1 hour.

Combine the red chile powder, cumin, paprika, oregano, and bay leaf in a heavy skillet and toast until the spices are brittle, but do not burn.

Heat the olive oil and sauté the onion, garlic, and bell pepper until soft. Add the spices and tomatoes and sauté 15 minutes. Add the remaining ingredients and enough water to make a loose consistency and simmer, covered, for 2 hours. Adjust the water if necessary. Uncover and simmer, stirring occasionally, until thickened. Remove the ham hock and bay leaf and serve in bowls garnished with sprigs of cilantro.

Serves: 8 to 10
Heat Scale: Medium

〰〰〰〰〰〰〰

SEAFOOD CHOWDER WITH A HABANERO ZIP

La Tour Restaurant, Park Hyatt Hotel, Chicago, Illinois

It may seem unusual that a restaurant with a four-star rating from the *Mobil Travel Guide* would serve hot and spicy dishes, but the credit for that goes to executive chef Charles Weber, whose repertoire includes many chile-based recipes. He says, "When developing recipes using chiles, I take into consideration the desired level of heat, other main ingredients and their particular flavors, and then the overall impact I want the chiles to have in the dish." He is particularly enamored of Habaneros, as evidenced by this recipe.

3   Tablespoons olive oil
1   medium carrot, peeled and chopped fine
2   ribs celery, chopped fine
1   Spanish onion, chopped fine
1   large potato, peeled and chopped fine
    corn kernels cut from 2 cobs
1   teaspoon ground cumin
1   teaspoon ground oregano
¼   cup light corn meal
1   cup white wine

1   **Habanero chile,** scored on the bottom (add more to increase the heat level if desired)
½   cup tomato paste
3   cups fish stock
2   cups mixed seafood, chopped (such as firm fish, shrimp, mussels, clams)
1   teaspoon fresh thyme, chopped

In a stockpot, sauté the carrots, celery, onion, potato, and corn in the olive oil for 5 minutes. Add the cumin, oregano, and corn meal and cook for 3 minutes over medium heat, stirring constantly. Add the wine and Habanero and cook for 3 or 4 minutes. Add the tomato paste and mix well, then add the fish stock, season lightly with salt and pepper, and simmer for 15 minutes.

Add the seafood and simmer for 15 minutes. Just before serving, stir in the fresh thyme.

Serves: 4 to 6
Heat Scale: Mild to Medium

EL PATIO'S POSOLE WITH CHILE CARIBE
El Patio, Albuquerque, New Mexico

Your editor confesses to having dined at this restaurant well over two hundred times, so maybe I'm a bit prejudiced when I say it's one of the top three New Mexican restaurants in the country. Chef Tom Baca refuses to compromise on heat and serves the hottest chiles he can find. He brushes off occasional complaints from burned-out customers, as if to say, if you can't take the heat, stay out of El Patio. Owner David Sandoval says he's powerless to do anything about the situation because Tom is not only his only chef, he's also his father-in-law! The following recipe is the proper way to make northern New Mexican-style *posole,* a winter holiday tradition.

THE POSOLE

2 **hot dried red New Mexican chiles,** stems and seeds removed

1 cup frozen or dried posole corn (hominy), which has been soaked in water overnight

1 teaspoon garlic powder

1 onion, chopped

3 cups water

1 pound pork loin, cut into 1-inch cubes

Combine all ingredients in a pot except the pork and boil at medium heat for about 3 hours or until the corn is tender, adding more water if necessary. Add the pork and continue cooking for 30 minutes, or until the pork is tender but not falling apart. The result should resemble a soup more than a stew.

CHILE CARIBE

6 hot dried red New Mexican   1 teaspoon garlic powder
chiles, stems and seeds
removed

Boil the chile pods in water for 15 minutes. Remove, add the garlic powder, and puree in a blender at high speed. Transfer to a serving bowl and allow to cool.

Note: For really hot chile caribe, add dried piquin, cayenne, or de arbol chiles to the mixture.

To serve: The posole should be served in soup bowls accompanied by warm flour tortillas. Three bowls of garnishes should be provided: the Chile Caribe, freshly minced cilantro, and freshly minced onion. Each guest can then adjust the pungency of the posole according to individual taste.

Serves: 4

Heat Scale: Varies according to amount of chile caribe added

ROCKERS IKO
Maple Leaf Grill, Seattle, Washington

Chef (he calls himself a cook) Rip Ripley was originally an archaeologist who began his culinary career "cooking for a camp of fifty hungry archaeologists in the middle of nowhere." Then he spent ten years as sous-chef at Seattle's Green Lake Grill, which prepared him for co-ownership (with David Albert) of the Maple Leaf. He refers to cooking with chiles as "edible art," and his philosophy of hot and spicy is: "If y'all don't sweat, then y'all ain't really et." This spicy seafood stew can be made hotter by increasing the amount of minced chiles used, or by switching to fresh Habaneros. Incidentally, "rockers" refers to the rockfish used and "Iko" was the song "Iko, Iko" that Rip was listening to when he invented the recipe.

IKO SAUCE

1 medium red onion, diced

1 medium red bell pepper, seeded and diced

1 Tablespoon olive oil

1 Tablespoon ground cumin

2 teaspoons ground coriander

1 teaspoon thyme

1 Tablespoon fresh ginger, diced

1 bay leaf

2 to 3 Tablespoons fresh hot chile pepper such as serrano, stemmed, seeded, and minced (or more to add heat)

1 teaspoon chopped fresh garlic

½ cup white wine

1 Tablespoon lemon juice

3 pounds tomatoes, peeled and chopped

Sauté the onion and bell pepper in the oil until soft. Add the spices, chile, and garlic and sauté 30 seconds to aromatize. Add the wine, lemon juice, and tomatoes, and simmer for 15 to 20 minutes.

IKO STEW

½ red bell pepper, julienned
1 carrot, julienned
2 stalks celery, julienned
1 leek, julienned
2 Tablespoons olive oil
   Iko Sauce

3 pounds seafood, including clams in their shells, mussels, crawfish, fish (rockfish, salmon, cod) cut into 1-inch squares, scallops, and shucked oysters

Sauté the vegetables in the oil. Add the Iko Sauce and simmer for a minute. Add the clams and when they begin to open, add the fish and simmer 3 to 4 minutes. Add the remainder of the seafood and simmer an additional 4 minutes or until done.

Serves: 6 to 8
Heat Scale: Medium

Marvelous Meats

In this health-conscious age, meat has been constantly under attack as being too high in fat and cholesterol. For a while, it looked like increasing fish and poultry consumption would turn cattle and pigs into endangered species. However, beef and pork producers have responded by producing much leaner meats than in the past, and meat consumption has started to rebound.

The only problem with leaner cuts of meat is that they lack fat, the primary flavoring ingredient. Experts claim that in blind taste-tests of fat-free meats, diners are unable to detect the difference between beef, pork, and lamb. So, if some fat is a necessity for producing delicious meat dishes, how do we justify consuming it?

The keys here are moderation and variation. We should not eat beef at every meal; likewise, we shouldn't exist solely on a daily diet of mung beans or tofu either. As long as we trim excess fat off of meats, eat them in moderation, and alternate them with other sources of protein, we should have few problems. Incidentally, Carol Ann Rinzler, author of *The Complete Book of Food*, writes that the most nutritious way to serve beef is with foods rich in vitamin C. Well, fresh green chile peppers have about twice the vitamin C as an orange.

Chefs around the country today are combining meats and chiles with abandon. In this chapter, we begin with variations on some American standards and then proceed to some culinary combinations that stretch the imagination.

MAD WILL'S BURGER THANG
Firehouse Bar-B-Que, Burlingame, California

The Firehouse, started in San Francisco in 1978 by a firefighter, is now located in Burlingame, about five miles south of the San Francisco Airport. It features ribs, chicken, sausage, and other barbecue specialties, slow-cooked in a brick oven. In addition to barbecue, Chef Mad Will Shapiro offers his version of an American staple—but considerably spiced up!

1	pound ground chuck	**4**	**slices jalapeño jack cheese**
1	**cup extra hot barbecue sauce***	**2**	**serrano chiles,** stems removed, seeded, and minced
½	onion, chopped fine	1	avocado, peeled, pitted, and sliced
2	cloves garlic, minced		
½	teaspoon cumin seeds	4	hamburger buns
½	**teaspoon cayenne powder**		

Combine the chuck, ½ cup of the barbecue sauce, onion, garlic, cumin seeds, and cayenne in a bowl and mix thoroughly. Form into four patties and grill until done. Just before serving, ladle some of the remaining barbecue sauce on each patty, followed by a slice of jack cheese, a sprinkling of serranos, and slices of avocado. Serve on buns that have been toasted over the coals.

Serves: 4
Heat Scale: Hot

*Mad Will, of course, uses Firehouse's own brand, Firehouse 3-Alarm Sauce.

QUAKER STEAK & LUBEBURGER
Quaker Steak & Lube, Sharon, Pennsylvania

Here is another spicy specialty burger. The Quaker Steak, housed in a former gas station, began in 1973 as a "cook your own steak" restaurant and now has gained a national reputation for its record sales of chicken wings. General manager Bob Mentrek would not disclose the recipes for their nine wing sauces, which range from "mild to suicide," but he did spring for the burger recipe.

2	teaspoons melted butter	4	slices American cheese
	garlic salt to taste	8	bacon strips
4	sesame seed buns	4	lettuce leaves
4	8-ounce hamburger patties, ⅔-inch thick	8	slices fresh tomato
		4	slices red onion
1-½	cups sautéed mushrooms	½	cup blue cheese dressing
½	**cup of your favorite bottled hot sauce**		

Mix the melted butter with the garlic salt and brush on the top side of the sliced bun.

Grill the burgers to desired doneness and, at the last minute, top each with the mushrooms, 2 tablespoons hot sauce, 1 slice of cheese, and 2 slices of bacon. While the cheese is melting, toast the buns on the grill.

Place the burgers on the buns and top with lettuce, tomato slices, onion slices, and blue cheese dressing.

Serves: 4
Heat Scale: Medium

BARBECUED BEEF BRISKET FIREHOUSE STYLE
Firehouse Bar-B-Que, Burlingame, California

Chef Mad Will Shapiro's favorite movie is "Some Like It Hot," with Marilyn Monroe, and his favorite song is Robert Palmer's "Some Like It Hot"! Here's his recipe for a classic barbecue specialty, beef brisket. Yes, it's simple enough, but it takes a lot of patience to cook it correctly.

1 beef brisket, untrimmed	**barbecue sauce,** such as
2-½ cups of extra hot	Firehouse 3-Alarm Sauce

Place the brisket fat side up in a glass dish. Slather on half of the barbecue sauce, cover with foil, and marinate at least four hours in the refrigerator (overnight is better).

Cook the brisket in your smoker or pit over indirect heat at 200 degrees for 12 hours. Baste the brisket with the remainder of the sauce during the process. It should be extremely tender when done. Serve with potato salad, corn on the cob, and cole slaw for a great summer barbecue.

Serves: 6 to 8
Heat Scale: Medium

〰〰〰〰〰〰〰

THE MEX FAJITAS
The Mex, Ellsworth, Maine

In 1979, Bruce and Sandra Wardwell abandoned their respective careers as a sociology teacher and a registered nurse to bring the tastes of the Southwest to the Northeast. They opened The Mex in Ellsworth, about fifteen miles from Acadia National Park, and soon tourists and locals both were flooding in, causing the Wardwells to expand their seating from 46 to over 150 people. Their variation on fajitas is interesting because the marinade differs from the traditional jalapeño juice and port wine mixture. Also, the beef is seared, not grilled.

1 **Tablespoon pasilla chile powder** (or substitute ancho or New Mexican)

2 **Tablespoons of your favorite hot sauce**

juice of 5 limes

½ cup vegetable oil

½ cup olive oil

1 Tablespoon ground cumin

1 Tablespoon oregano

1 Tablespoon black pepper

2 teaspoons salt

2 to 3 pounds your choice of sliced boneless chicken breast, flank steak sliced across the grain, shrimp, scallops, fish steaks or fillets, or sliced tofu

½ cup diced onions

½ cup diced bell peppers

½ cup diced tomatoes

6 to 8 large flour tortillas

Combine the first 9 ingredients in a nonreactive bowl and add the meat or tofu of choice, but *do not* combine several choices in the same bowl. Marinate overnight in the refrigerator.

Place the strips in a very hot cast iron skillet, keeping them separate so they will sear, not steam. Add the onion, peppers, and tomatoes. Turn the strips once and cook until desired doneness. (Cut a strip open to check.)

Serve with warm flour tortillas and suggest that guests roll their own sandwich and add fresh salsa, guacamole, or sour cream as additional ingredients. Fajitas are often accompanied by Spanish rice and re-fried beans.

Serves: 6 to 8
Heat Scale: Medium

GUISADO NORTEÑO
El Norteño, Albuquerque, New Mexico

Owner Leo Nuñez notes that many American cookbooks written on Mexican cuisine insist that "guisado" only means "stew." It can be other dishes as well, as this simple but delicious recipe shows. He suggests, "Serve it with beans, rice, a little lettuce and tomato, and hot corn tortillas. A cold beer would be nice." Here is a south-of-the-border variation on fried pork chops.

4 center-cut pork chops, cut thin
  prepared mustard

Tomatillo Salsa (see recipe, page 38)

Heat a skillet or griddle, and while it is coming to temperature, slather mustard on one side of the chops and the salsa on the other. Sauté until juicy, turning once, and do not overcook. The trick is to get the meat chewy and juicy, but not dry. Serve with the salsa side up and with a side dish of the same salsa.

Serves: 2
Heat Scale: Mild

GRILLED FLANK STEAK WITH PECANS, BLACK BEANS, AND FRESH CILANTRO
Routh Street Café, Dallas, Texas

Stephan Pyles, owner and chef of the Routh Street Café, spends quite a bit of time in Mexico checking out chiles. "I find myself getting braver in my use of chiles," he says, "but I have to keep it in check because of the customers. With the intensity of chile flavors, I am finding that salt and fat are not needed to give great tastes to food."

1-½   cup plus ⅓ cup dry red wine
¾   cup corn oil
2   Tablespoons soy sauce
3   Tablespoons freshly
       chopped cilantro
**2   jalapeño chiles, stems
       removed, chopped with
       the seeds**
5   cloves garlic, 3 chopped
1   Tablespoon coarsely cracked
       black pepper
1   flank steak, 1-½ to 2 pounds
⅓   cup pecan halves
1   cup plus 2-½ Tablespoons
       unsalted butter

**4   serrano or 2 jalapeño
       chiles, stems and seeds
       removed, diced**
1   Tablespoon minced chives
⅓   cup chicken stock or canned
       broth
⅓   cup red wine vinegar
1   large shallot, chopped
1   teaspoon fresh lime juice
¼   cup canned or cooked black
       beans, drained and rinsed
       salt and freshly ground
       black pepper
       warm flour tortillas, as
       accompaniment

Combine 1-½ cups of the wine, the oil, soy sauce, 2 tablespoons of the cilantro, chopped jalapeños with the seeds, 3 cloves of chopped garlic, and the cracked black pepper. Marinate the flank steak in the mixture, in a nonaluminum pan, in the refrigerator overnight.

Toast the pecans in a 350 degree oven for 5 minutes until lightly browned. Remove from the oven and set aside.

Rub the remaining 2 whole garlic cloves with ½ tablespoon of the butter and roast in the oven until soft and light brown, about 20 minutes. Reduce the oven temperature to 250 degrees.

Crush together the pecans, roasted garlic, and serrano chiles. Blend in 2 tablespoons of the butter and the chives.

Combine the stock, remaining ⅓ cup wine, vinegar, shallot, and 1 teaspoon of the cilantro in a nonaluminum saucepan. Bring to a boil over moderate heat and boil until reduced to 2 tablespoons, about 10 to 12 minutes. Reduce the heat to low and whisk in the remaining 1 cup butter. Stir in the remaining 2 teaspoons of cilantro and the lime juice. Whisk in the pecan mixture. Stir in the black beans and season the sauce with salt and pepper to taste. Transfer the sauce to a double boiler and keep warm over simmering water.

Lightly brush the flank steak with oil. Season with salt and pepper. Grill the steak over a moderately hot fire or broil until medium rare, 5 to 7 minutes.

Thinly slice the steak crosswise on the diagonal and arrange on warmed plates. Spoon the sauce over each serving and accompany with warm flour tortillas.

Serves: 4 to 6
Heat Scale: Medium

~~~~~~~~~~~~~~~~

VENISON ADOBADA RAVIOLI WITH CHIVA CREMA AND SALSA VERDE
La Casa Sena, Santa Fe, New Mexico

La Casa Sena was built by Major José Sena in the late 1860s in the classic adobe style and is now on the National Historic Register. The historic architecture, combined with its extensive collections of Southwest, Indian, and Taos art combine to give the restaurant an elegant yet warm ambience. The restaurant uses seventeen different varieties of chiles. This intricate recipe is an example of combining the best native techniques with American regional styles and international accents. Not only is this dish pleasing to the palate, it is also pleasing visually.

THE VENISON

3 Tablespoons flour
2 Tablespoons butter
2 cups water
8 **Tablespoons red New Mexican chile powder**
1 **Tablespoon chile caribe** (crushed red chile)
1 **red jalapeño,** seeded, stemmed, and minced
1 pinch minced garlic
½ Tablespoon fresh oregano, chopped
   salt to taste
6 ounces minced venison

Make a roux with the the butter and flour, then add the other ingredients (except the venison) to make a chile sauce. Cook for 20 minutes, then add the venison and braise until tender. Allow to cool.

CHILE RAVIOLI

6 Tablespoons red chile powder
2 cups semolina flour
   pinch of salt

3 eggs
2 egg yolks, slightly beaten
   (reserve for assembly stage)

Mix all ingredients together except the egg yolks and knead to a firm consistency. Roll out to ⅛-inch thickness and cut into squares.

CHIVA CREMA

1 quart heavy cream
½ teaspoon minced garlic
1 Tablespoon basil, chopped
½ Tablespoon sage, chopped

2 white scallions, chopped
½ cup white wine
4 ounces goat cheese
   salt and pepper to taste

Reduce all ingredients over medium heat, adding the cheese and salt last.

Yield: 3 cups

SALSA VERDE

1 cucumber, chopped fine
1 bunch scallion greens, chopped
1 bunch cilantro, chopped
4 tomatillos, chopped
¼ cup butter

¼ cup white wine
1 quart heavy cream, reduced by half
   juice of 1 lime
   salt and pepper to taste

Sear the cucumber, scallions, cilantro, and tomatillos in a pan with the butter and wine. Remove from heat, cool slightly, and puree in a blender until absolutely smooth. Return puree to the pan, add the remaining ingredients, and simmer until thick.

Yield: 2-½ cups

To assemble and serve: Place the venison mixture on the ravioli squares and fold into triangles. Seal the edges of the raviolis by painting the corners with the egg yolks. Poach the raviolis for 6 to 8 minutes. To serve, spread the Chiva Crema over an entire plate, then make a concentric circle with the Salsa Verde. Place the raviolis atop the sauces. For an added touch, outline the dish with a thin circle of red chile sauce.

Serves: 6
Heat Scale: Medium

~~~~~~~~~~~~~~~~~~~~

VENISON STEAKS WITH CRANBERRY-CHIPOTLE SAUCE
Routh Street Café, Dallas, Texas

"I'm particularly fond of chipotle chiles because of their color, texture, and flavor," says chef and co-owner Stephan Pyles. "They give my sauces a wonderful color. And the smoky taste adds another dimension to the underlying flavor of food. They make a wonderful barbecue sauce. They are also great combined with cumin and roasted tomatoes as a sauce for game and any dark meat."

4	Tablespoons clarified butter or vegetable oil	2-½	cups reduced venison stock (or substitute beef stock)
4	venison loin steaks, about 4 ounces each salt to taste	**1**	**Tablespoon pureed chipotles in adobo sauce**
2	Tablespoons minced shallots	1	teaspoon fresh sage, chopped
2	cloves garlic, minced		
2	cups cranberries	3	Tablespoons whole butter at room temperature
3	Tablespoons sugar	4	sage leaves for garnish
1	cup dry red wine		

Heat the butter in a large skillet over medium heat. Season the steaks with salt to taste and sauté them for 1-½ minutes per side. Remove them from the pan and keep warm while making the sauce.

Pour off all but 1 tablespoon of the butter, add the shallots and garlic, and cook for 20 seconds. Add the cranberries and sugar and cook for 30 seconds longer.

Deglaze the pan with the wine and reduce by ¾ over high heat. Add the stock and chipotle puree and sage. Reduce by ⅓ and strain through a fine sieve. Return to a clean saucepan and heat to boiling. Whisk in the butter and remove from heat.

Serve the sauce over the steaks with a sage leaf as garnish.

Serves: 4
Heat Scale: Medium

∼∿∿∿∿∿∿∿∼

SMOKED JAMAICAN JERK RIBS
Majestic Diner, Austin, Texas

Self-taught chef Mick Vann believes that hot and spicy food is a necessity in the hot climate of Austin. "It keeps you cooler and makes you sweat," he says. "Besides, hot and spicy is healthier, fresher, and much less boring than northern latitude cooking." The following recipe of Mick's won the People's Choice Award in the 1991 Hill Country Food and Wine Festival.

6   yellow onions, coarsely chopped

3   bunches green onions, coarsely chopped

3   cups fresh orange juice

½   cup fresh lime juice

½   cup orange juice concentrate

6   Scotch bonnet (Habanero) chiles, stems removed

3   Tablespoons cayenne powder

6   Tablespoons ground allspice

6   Tablespoons thyme

3   Tablespoons fine black pepper

3   Tablespoons rubbed sage

4-½   teaspoons nutmeg

4-½   teaspoons cinnamon

2-¼   cups soy sauce

¾	cup granulated sugar	4-½	cups white vinegar
6	Tablespoons brown sugar	1-½	cups Meyer's Dark Rum
1-½	cups olive oil	6	pounds pork ribs

Combine the onions, juices, and chiles in a food processor and puree. Add the remaining ingredients except the ribs and puree until smooth. The marinade yield is about a quart and it will keep in the refrigerator for about 2 weeks.

Steam the ribs on racks, about 45 minutes for baby back ribs and 70 minutes for short ribs. Marinate the ribs in the jerk sauce for at least 1 hour, and preferably overnight.

Smoke the ribs over a mild wood such as pecan or apple. Use low heat and smoke for at least an hour.

Serves: 6
Heat Scale: Hot

〰〰〰〰〰〰

POBLANO CHILE-STUFFED FILET MIGNON
On the Verandah, Highlands, North Carolina

Alan and Marta Figel love to travel and collect recipes and recipe ideas for their eclectic menu at On the Verandah. Undoubtedly, this recipe was influenced by their visits to Mexico, the chief producer of the mild and tasty poblano, which is known as "ancho" in its dried form.

4	**poblano chiles,** stems removed, roasted, peeled and seeded, and chopped fine	½	cup grated Monterey Jack cheese
1	cup chopped onion	3	Tablespoons dry bread crumbs
2	cloves garlic, minced	2-½	pounds beef tenderloin, cut into 6 slices 1 inch thick
2	Tablespoons vegetable oil		

Sauté the chiles, onion, and garlic in the oil until tender. Turn off the heat and add the cheese and bread crumbs.

Cut deep pockets in the edges of the steaks and season lightly with salt and pepper. Put 2 tablespoons of stuffing in each pocket and close the pockets with toothpicks.

Grill the steaks 4 to 5 minutes each side for medium rare.

Serves: 6
Heat Scale: Mild

POBLANO CHILES STUFFED WITH PORT-SALUT AND CRISPY LAMB
L.A. Nicola Restaurant, Los Angeles, California

Chef Larry Nicola has lamb grown especially for his restaurant on a ranch in Arizona, and he buys his chiles directly from growers in the town of Tubac in that same state. It is evident that he cares a lot about the quality of ingredients in the dishes he creates. This recipe is his version of *chiles rellenos*.

TOMATILLO-CILANTRO SAUCE

6 tomatillos, quartered	¼ cup fresh cilantro leaves
2 cloves garlic, chopped	2 cups water

Place all ingredients in a pan and simmer until the tomatillos are very soft. Keep the sauce warm.

Yield: 2 cups

THE STUFFED CHILES

12 ounces lamb leg meat, cut into thin strips

2 cloves whole garlic

2 Tablespoons olive oil

4 poblano chiles, stems removed, roasted, peeled, and seeded (remove the seeds through a small slit in the top of each pod)

12 ounces Port-Salut cheese, cut into strips

2 eggs

¼ cup milk

several Tablespoons flour

10 sprigs mint for garnish freshly cooked tortilla chips for garnish

Sauté the lamb and garlic in the oil and then place the cooked strips of lamb inside the chiles. Save the oil. Cut the cheese into strips and place inside the chiles.

Mix together the eggs and milk. Dust the chiles with flour, dip them in the egg-milk mixture, and then sauté them in the reserved oil, turning once, until golden brown.

To serve, spoon the tomatillo sauce into the bottom of each plate. Place the chiles on top of the sauce and garnish with the mint and tortilla chips.

Serves: 4
Heat Scale: Mild

CLASSIC CARNE ADOBADO
Pecos River Café, New York, New York

Just because this restaurant is located in the Big Apple, don't think for a minute that it's not authentic. Chef and cookbook author Jane Butel spent years in New Mexico learning to cook its cuisine and returns every summer to Santa Fe to conduct cooking classes. Here is a traditional New Mexican dish, *carne adobado* (sometimes spelled "adovada"), in a quantity large enough for a party.

1 **cup chile caribe** (crushed hot red pods)

4 cups water

2 teaspoons salt

3 cloves garlic, chopped

2 Tablespoons Mexican oregano

2 Tablespoons ground cumin

5 pounds pork shoulder chops (1 inch thick)

Combine the chile caribe and the water in a blender and process until well blended. Add the salt, garlic, oregano, and cumin and mix well.

Trim the excess fat from the pork, leaving at least ¼-inch, and place the slices in a flat baking dish. Cover the pork with the sauce and turn once to coat evenly on both sides. If possible, marinate in the refrigerator overnight.

To cook, place the pork chops in a baking dish, cover with a lid or aluminum foil, and bake at 325 degrees for 30 minutes. Uncover and bake for 30 minutes more.

Shred the meat from the bones and mix with the sauce remaining in the dish,

Serve over corn tortillas, softened by frying in oil for a few seconds. Top with grated cheddar cheese if desired.

Serves: 10 or more

Heat Scale: Hot

MEAT CURRIED WITH GARAM MASALA

Sim's Catering, Washington, New Jersey

Among the hot sauces, salsas, spicy condiments, and various dried and fresh chiles available at Sim's is one of owner Sim Baron's favorite cooking ingredients, *garam masala.* "Note that no curry powder is used in this recipe," he says. "Instead, a *garam masala,* which has hundreds of variations and translates loosely as "heating spice mixture," is the main seasoning. This aromatic mix may be purchased at Indian food suppliers, or it may be made at home by following a recipe from a good Indian cookbook." A typical *garam masala* combines ground red chiles, black pepper, cumin seed, cinnamon, cloves, mace, cardamom, coriander, and bay leaf, all ground together until very fine.

1	medium yellow onion, chopped	**2**	**teaspoons *garam masala***
1	large bell pepper, seeded and diced	1	teaspoon ground turmeric
4	cloves garlic, minced	2	teaspoons salt
1-½	teaspoons ground ginger	1	pound lean red meat (beef, lamb, venison, or pork), cut into 1-inch cubes
1	Tablespoon butter or vegetable oil	3	medium tomatoes
½	**teaspoon ground cayenne**	1	cup water

Sauté the onions, bell pepper, garlic, and ginger in the butter or oil until the vegetables are soft. Add the cayenne, *garam masala,* turmeric, and salt, mix well, and sauté for 2 minutes.

Add the meat and stir well to coat. Cover loosely and cook over low heat for 30 minutes. If the meat gets too dry, add a couple of tablespoons of water. Add the tomatoes and raise the heat to fry for 3 minutes. Add the water, bring to a boil, then reduce the heat and simmer for about 30 minutes or until the meat is very tender.

Check the consistency of the sauce—it should be thick. If not, raise the heat to thicken the sauce. Serve over rice.

Serves: 4
Heat Scale: Medium

RED CHILE PEPPER PUREE WITH PORK AND FRIED PLANTAINS

L.A. Nicola Restaurant, Los Angeles, California

A native Angeleno of Lebanese extraction, chef Larry Nicola literally grew up in the family's Nicola Twins Market, so he appreciates fresh ingredients, especially chile peppers. Interestingly enough, his restaurant is in the same neighborhood where the market used to be. About this recipe, Larry advises: "Pour some beer and have a good time!"

10 red New Mexican chile pods, stems and seeds removed	3-pound leg of pork
	12 cloves garlic
1 quart water	2 plantains
salt and pepper to taste	¼ cup olive oil

Boil the chiles in the water for fifteen minutes. Puree the pods in a blender, then strain through a sieve to remove any pieces of skin. Add salt and pepper to taste.

Stud the leg of pork with 10 garlic cloves. Pour the chile puree over the leg and roast at 350 degrees for 2 hours.

Slice the plantains lengthwise and sauté with 2 cloves of garlic in the olive oil until golden. Serve the pork garnished with the fried plantains.

Serves 4
Heat Scale: Medium

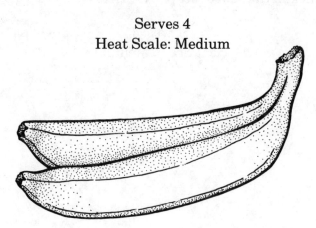

ROAST RACK OF LAMB
WITH BELL PEPPER COULIS AND
TOMATILLO-JALAPEÑO SAUCE
Restaurant Muse, Hermosa Beach, California

This "clean and very simple restaurant" has made great strides in the nine years it has been open. "We have survived successfully," says chef Vaughn Allen, who adds that he appreciates the flavor of the chiles in his recipes as much as the heat. Some of the celebrity diners at Restaurant Muse include Madonna, David Bowie, Raquel Welch, David Lynch, and Janet Jackson.

THE LAMB
1 Frenched rack of lamb
1 bunch fresh rosemary, minced
6 cloves garlic, chopped
1 teaspoon cracked black pepper
2 Tablespoons olive oil

Rub the lamb with a mixture of the rosemary, 6 garlic cloves, and pepper and brush with olive oil. Let sit for several hours.

BELL PEPPER COULIS
1 red bell pepper, roasted and
     peeled
1 shallot, peeled
1 clove garlic, peeled
1 egg yolk
¼ cup champagne vinegar
⅓ cup extra virgin olive oil

Puree the bell pepper, shallot, garlic clove, and egg together. Add the vinegar and puree again. While running the food processor, remove the top and slowly add the olive oil. Season the coulis with salt and pepper to taste and set aside.

Yield: 1 cup

TOMATILLO-JALAPEÑO SAUCE

1 cup water
1 jalapeño (or more to taste), stem removed, halved, and seeded
6 tomatillos, husks removed

1 small Spanish onion, quartered
1 clove garlic, minced
whole chives and buttered baby carrots for garnish

Place the water, jalapeño, tomatillos, onion, and minced garlic in a small saucepan and bring to a boil. Reduce heat and simmer for ten minutes. Drain, cool to room temperature, and chop coarsely. Set aside.

Yield: 1-½ cups

To serve: In a 400 degree oven, roast the lamb on the fat side for 15 minutes. Turn and roast for another 10 minutes. Remove from the oven and slice the rack.

Spread the coulis on a plate, arrange the sliced lamb over it, and top with the tomatillo-jalapeño sauce. Garnish with the chives and baby carrots.

Serves: 4 to 6
Heat Scale: Mild

~~~~~~~~~~

PORK PARMESAN WITH ORANGE AND ANCHO CHILE SAUCE

Jeffrey's, Austin, Texas

A sophisticated dining experience in a laid-back atmosphere is what Jeffrey's offers. Consistently ranked as one of Austin's best restaurants, Jeffrey's serves regional Southwestern cuisine as designed by executive chef Raymond Tatum, who is famous for his sauces.

1-½ pounds pork tenderloin, cut into 6 4-ounce medallions
salt and pepper
1-½ cups grated Parmesan cheese
¼ cup milk
3 eggs
4 ancho chiles, stems removed and seeded
1 cup flour

2 Tablespoons crushed red chile
¼ cup cooking oil
¼ cup clarified butter
½ cup chicken stock
¼ cup orange juice
5 Tablespoons lemon juice
¾ cup butter
4 blood oranges, peeled and sectioned

Pound out the pork tenderloins until they are ¼ inch thick and season with salt and pepper.

Mix together the cheese, milk, eggs, crushed chile flakes, and ½ cup of the flour. The batter should not be runny.

Fry the anchos in the cooking oil for about 30 seconds, remove from heat, and chop fine. Add the clarified butter to a nonstick skillet. Dust the medallions with the remaining flour, dip in the batter, and cook over medium heat until the batter becomes firm and golden brown on both sides. Remove and place in a 350 degree oven on a cookie sheet for 5 to 7 minutes.

In a saucepan, reduce the chicken stock, orange juice, and lemon juice together until about ½ cup remains. Whisk in the ¾ cup butter. Over moderate heat, add the anchos and the orange sections. Serve this sauce over the pork.

Serves: 6
Heat Scale: Medium

Savory Seafood

Many people are surprised to learn that the combination of chiles and seafood is not just the result of the wave of interest in hot and spicy foods that began in this country more than a decade ago. Chile-flavored seafoods have been around for thousands of years, though they were chronicled only after the Europeans arrived in the New World. In 1529, the Spanish friar and historian, Bernardino de Sahagún, noted that the Native Americans in what is now Mexico "would eat another kind of stew, with frogs and green chile, and a stew of *axolotl* (salamander) with yellow chile." Fortunately, we have tastier seafood available these days.

As chile peppers spread around the world during the sixteenth century, they were readily incorporated into the cuisines of many countries and combined with foods that were already being consumed. Some of the classic combinations of chile and seafood include Singapore chile crab, prawns in red chile from

Thailand, and lobster with chiles, citrus, and cashews from China.

Here in the United States, chefs are continuing, and even expanding, the tradition of hot and spicy seafood by contrasting the relative blandness of most seafood (when compared to meat or poultry) with the spicy, exotic flavors of numerous varieties of chiles. We see shrimp combined with jalapeños and anchos, crab with New Mexican chiles, chipotles with salmon, and scallops or swordfish mated with Habaneros.

Because one of the earliest spicy seafood creations is the blend of raw seafood and hot chiles, we begin with two versions of *ceviche*.

COMPADRES CEVICHE

Compadres Mexican Bar and Grill, Honolulu, Hawaii

In addition to its Hawaiian restaurants, there are Compadres in San Francisco, Palo Alto, Sacramento, and the Napa Valley. Ceviche, of course, is seafood that is "cooked" in acidic lime juice. There are dozens and dozens of variations of this dish from Baja California south to Chile, and this version, by executive chef Alfonso Navarro, is one of the most interesting.

2 pounds combination firm white fish and scallops, cut into small cubes
fresh lime juice
1 large onion, diced
2 serrano chiles (or more to taste), stems removed, seeded, and minced
¼ **cup New Mexican green chile,** chopped

¼ cup olive oil
1 teaspoon Mexican oregano
¼ small bunch cilantro, minced
½ pound Dungeness crab meat, shredded
2 tomatoes, peeled, seeded, and diced
5 radishes, sliced in semicircles
½ avocado, peeled, pitted, and diced

Place the fish and scallops in a ceramic bowl and cover them with lime juice. Cover the bowl and refrigerate for at least four hours or until the fish becomes opaque. Add the onion, chiles, olive oil, oregano, cilantro, and crab and mix lightly. Refrigerate for 1 hour.

Just before serving, stir in the tomatoes, radishes, and avocado. Serve in tall, stemmed glasses.

Serves: 12 in 4-ounce portions
Heat Scale: Mild to Medium

THE MEX SEVICHE
The Mex, Ellsworth, Maine

"Our passion for cooking an exciting, different, healthy, and satisfying cuisine is alive and thriving!" say Bruce and Sandy Wardwell of The Mex, one of our northernmost Hot Spots. They have traveled extensively in Mexico researching recipes. In their version of marinated and spiced raw seafood, the Wardwells use lemons in addition to limes.

⅓ **cup pickled jalapeños,** seeds and stems removed, chopped

⅓ **cup juice from the pickled jalapeños**

2 to 3 pounds haddock fillets or other mild white fish, cut into large chunks

juice of 5 lemons

juice of 10 limes

⅔ cup cider vinegar

2 teaspoons salt

3 tomatoes, diced

2 bell peppers, seeds removed, diced

1 Spanish onion, diced

Combine the first 7 ingredients in a nonreactive bowl or jar and refrigerate 24 to 36 hours.

Shortly before serving, add the remaining ingredients and toss well. Serve chilled on a bed of greens.

Serves: 6 to 8
Heat Scale: Medium

SPICY FISH CARIBE ON PASTA
W. C. Longacre Catering Company, Albuquerque, New Mexico

Chef W.C., formerly of the late, lamented Portside Restaurant in Key West, is taking a break between restaurants by operating his own catering company. Since his culinary training was influenced by stints in New Mexico, Hong Kong, and Key West, when asked what kind of cuisine he prepares, he answers with a straight face: "New Hong Key, of course."

TERIYAKI-CHILE MARINADE

1-½ **Tablespoons red New Mexican chile molido** (coarsely ground red chile powder)

1 cup teriyaki sauce

½ bunch fresh parsley, chopped

1 cup dry white wine
juice of 1 lemon

3 Tablespoons peeled and shredded ginger root

Combine all ingredients in a bowl.

Yield: 2-½ cups

SPICY FISH CARIBE

2 pounds fish fillets cut into 1-inch cubes (snapper preferred)

Teriyaki-Chile Marinade

6 Tablespoons peanut oil

2 Tablespoons peeled and shredded ginger root

½ **Tablespoon red New Mexican chile molido**

4 carrots, peeled and shredded

2 red bell peppers, seeded and chopped

1 small onion, chopped fine

¾ cup fresh peas (or substitute frozen)

1 pound fettuccine, cooked *al dente* and lightly tossed in vegetable oil

orange wedges for garnish

Marinate the fish for one hour, turning every 15 minutes. Remove from the marinade and drain.

Heat the peanut oil in a wok or large sauté pan to medium-high heat, add the ginger, chile, and fish, turning immediately. Add the carrots, bell peppers, onion, and peas. Cook for three minutes, then add ¼ cup marinade. Reduce heat, cover and cook for 2 minutes.

Bring the remaining marinade to a boil in a large saucepan and mix in the fettuccine until it is hot. Top the fettuccine with the fish and garnish with orange wedges.

Serves: 4 to 6
Heat Scale: Medium

∿∿∿∿∿∿∿∿∿∿

LOUISIANE SMOTHERED SHRIMP
McKinnon's Louisiane Restaurant, Atlanta, Georgia

Owner Billy McKinnon became hooked on hot and spicy foods nearly twenty years ago when he hired a Thai dishwasher who subsequently became a cook. He says that most of the food served in the restaurant is New Orleans Creole, but he has made sure that some spicy Cajun dishes were on the menu. This shrimp dish is an amalgam of Southern and Southwestern styles.

4 Tablespoons sweet butter
1 large onion, chopped
2 cloves garlic, minced
1 **poblano chile,** stem removed, roasted, peeled, seeded, and diced
1 **large jalapeño,** stem removed, minced
1 red bell pepper, seeded and julienned
1 green bell pepper, seeded and julienned
cooked corn cut off of 2 ears
1 cup heavy cream
1 pound medium shrimp, peeled and deveined
4 cups cooked rice
2 small bunches cilantro, chopped

Sauté the onions, garlic, chiles, and bell peppers in butter. In a separate pan, add the corn to the cream and reduce by one-third. Add the shrimp to the vegetables and sauté for 2 minutes. Add the corn and cream and simmer 2 more minutes.

Make a ring of rice around each plate and serve the shrimp mixture inside. Garnish with the cilantro.

Serves: 4
Heat Scale: Mild

∿∿∿∿∿∿∿∿∿∿

BLUE CORN CRAB TOSTADA
Piñon Grill, The Inn at McCormick Ranch, Scottsdale, Arizona

Executive Chef Farn Boggie combines ingredients indigenous to the Southwest in classically prepared dishes to create his own version of Southwestern cuisine. He feels that "the wide variety of chile peppers available in this market offers endless possibilities for intriguing new dishes." His version of tostadas is a case in point.

4 blue corn tortillas
1 Tablespoon butter
1 **New Mexican green chile,** stem and seeds removed, cut into julienne strips
1 clove garlic, minced
4 ounces snow crab meat
½ teaspoon cumin

½ **teaspoon red chile powder**
4 ounces boursin cheese, grated shredded lettuce for garnish
1 cup tomatoes, peeled, seeded, and diced
½ avocado cut in ⅛-inch slices

Place each tortilla in a tostada holder and deep fry to form a tostada shell. Set aside.

In a skillet, sauté the green chile and garlic in the butter for about a minute. The chile should stay firm. Add the crab meat, cumin, and chile powder and sauté for another minute. Stir in the cheese until melted.

Place the lettuce, tomatoes, and avocado evenly on the 4 tostada shells. Spoon the crab meat mixture evenly over the shells. Serve with Fresh Tomato-Peach Salsa (see recipe, page 35) or a salsa of your choice.

Serves: 4
Heat Scale: Mild

∿∿∿∿∿∿∿∿∿∿∿∿

SCALLOPS WITH CURRIED CHICK PEA SAUCE
Jay's Café at Clinton Hall, Ithaca, New York

Jay's Café specializes in tropical cuisine, particularly the dishes of the Caribbean and Pacific Rim. Jay Solomon, owner and chef, is the author of *Condiments!* (Crossing Press, 1990) and is a confirmed chile aficionado. "I'm into waking up people's palates," he says, and proves it with his recipes, which include Scotch bonnet (Habanero) chiles, the hottest of the hot.

2 Tablespoons butter	½ teaspoon black pepper
1 medium red onion, diced	¼ teaspoon salt
1 medium red bell pepper, chopped fine	2 sweet potatoes, scrubbed and chopped
2 cloves garlic, minced	2 cups water
2 teaspoons minced fresh ginger	1 can chick peas (garbanzo beans)
1 Scotch bonnet (Habanero) chile, stem removed, seeded and minced	2 Tablespoons butter
2 Tablespoons curry powder	2 pounds sea scallops, washed
1 teaspoon ground cumin	1 cup cooked okra, chopped
½ teaspoon ground cloves	

Sauté the onion, bell pepper, garlic, ginger, and Scotch bonnet in the butter in a deep skillet for 5 or 6 minutes over medium heat. Add the curry powder, cumin, cloves, black pepper, and salt and sauté for another 2 minutes. Add the sweet potatoes and water and simmer for about 15 minutes, or until the sweet potatoes are soft. Lower the heat, add the chick peas, and cook for another 10 minutes. Remove this sauce from the heat and set aside.

In another skillet, sauté the scallops in the remaining butter over moderately high heat for 10 to 12 minutes. Add the okra, cook for another 2 minutes, and then add the chick pea sauce. Simmer for 4 to 5 minutes, stirring frequently.

Serve the curried scallops over Caribbean peas and rice.

Serves: 4
Heat Scale: Medium

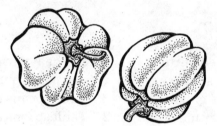

SEAFOOD COU-COU
The Pickled Parrot, Minneapolis, Minnesota

Imagine a restaurant that features an eclectic mix of Southwestern, Cuban, and Caribbean foods with an emphasis on chiles and uses the slogan, "The Heat Is On!" Then crank up your imagination one more notch and picture this restaurant in Minneapolis! Yes indeed, the Pickled Parrot is evidence of the continuing spread of chiles and ethnic cuisines. The menu includes such diverse dishes as Red Chile Pasta with Crab, Cream of Jalapeño Soup, and Jamaican Jerk Burgers. Below is one of executive chef Mitch Omer's favorite recipes.

COU-COU

¼	cup minced green onions	½	stick butter
½	large red onion, minced	½	Tablespoon kosher salt
½	large red bell pepper, stem and seeds removed, minced	1	quart rich chicken stock
		1-½	cups white cornmeal
1	**jalapeño chile,** stem and seeds removed, minced	2	cups grated Parmesan cheese
2	cloves garlic, minced		

Sauté the green onions, red onions, bell pepper, jalapeño, and garlic in the butter for about 1 minute, then season with the salt and set aside.

Bring the chicken stock to a boil and gradually add the cornmeal while stirring constantly. Slowly stir in the Parmesan cheese, reduce heat and cook, stirring constantly, for 20 minutes.

Fold in the sautéed mixture and blend well. Pour the mixture into a well-greased cookie sheet and refrigerate for at least 5 hours.

SEAFOOD COU-COU PREPARATION

2	teaspoons unsalted butter	⅓	cup heavy whipping cream
1	teaspoon minced shallots	2	teaspoons pure vanilla extract
2	teaspoons minced garlic	3	Tablespoons coconut rum
2	ounces raw lobster meat, coarsely chopped	2	Tablespoons coconut milk
2	ounces fresh bay scallops, coarsely chopped	2	Tablespoons julienned leek
			Cou-Cou
2	ounces peeled and deveined shrimp, coarsely chopped		olive oil
½	**teaspoon ground chile de árbol**	4	whole crawfish, poached

Prepare hot coals for grilling.

Sauté the shallots, garlic, and seafood pieces in the butter for about 1 minute over high heat. Pour off any excess butter and add the chile, cream, vanilla, coconut rum, and coconut milk. Simmer until slightly thickened and add the leek.

While the seafood is simmering, cut the Cou-Cou into squares 3 inches on a side. Brush the squares with olive oil and grill them until they are heated through, about 1 minute a side. Take care not to burn the Cou-Cou.

Top the Cou-Cou with the seafood mixture and garnish each with a crawfish.

Serves: 4 to 6
Heat Scale: Mild

CILANTRO-GRILLED SCALLOPS WITH GREEN CHILE BEURRE BLANC AND RED AND GREEN CHILE FETTUCCINE
Restaurant André, Albuquerque, New Mexico

Chef André Diddy wanted to take cooking out of the dark, so he made the kitchen the display centerpiece of his establishment. All of the cooking is done "on stage," in front of the customers. Chef Diddy loves to prepare game and buys the finest local produce and regional specialties, such as chile peppers, blue corn, piñon nuts, and wild mushrooms.

RED AND GREEN CHILE PASTAS
The recipes are identical—only the chiles change. It is best to prepare the pasta the day before, then cover and refrigerate.

½ **cup red jalapeños or New Mexican green chile,** stems removed, roasted, peeled, seeded, and chopped fine

2 cups semolina flour
2 cups all-purpose flour
2 eggs
2 Tablespoons olive oil

Puree the chile in a food processor and save in a separate bowl. Place all the other ingredients in a food processor and blend until mixed. Add the chile puree and process until the mixture holds together. If too soft, add more semolina flour. Remove and knead the dough into a ball, and leave at room temperature for 2 hours.

Cut the dough into three pieces, dust each with flour, and roll out into thin sheets. Cut the sheets into long noodles with a sharp knife, or use a pasta machine.

SCALLOPS AND BEURRE BLANC

4	Tablespoons lime juice		1-½	pounds large sea scallops
1	teaspoon cracked black pepper		2	sticks unsalted butter, diced
4	Tablespoons Chardonnay wine		1	**cup New Mexican green chiles,** roasted, peeled, seeded, and chopped fine
2	Tablespoons white vinegar		¼	teaspoon turmeric
¼	cup finely minced shallots			Red and Green Chile Pastas
8	sprigs cilantro, finely minced			olive oil
				cilantro for garnish

Combine the first six ingredients in a glass bowl, add the scallops, and marinate for 15 minutes. Drain the scallops and reserve the liquid in a saucepan. Bring the reserved liquid to a boil and reduce the volume to one-third of the original amount. Reduce the heat to a simmer, whisk in the butter, and add the green chile and turmeric. Keep this Beurre Blanc warm.

Broil or grill the scallops for 2 minutes per side. Keep warm.

Boil the pastas together for 3 minutes in lightly salted, rapidly boiling water. Drain the pastas and toss with olive oil. Place the pastas in the middle of each plate, surround with the Green Chile Beurre Blanc, place the scallops in the sauce, and garnish with cilantro leaves.

Serves: 4
Heat Scale: Medium

PRAWNS WITH ANCHO CHILE, TEQUILA, LIME, AND GARLIC
Miss Pearl's Jam House, San Francisco, California

Seafood is paramount at Miss Pearl's. Chef Joey Altman's menus offer a fish-of-the-day for breakfast, grilled snapper sandwiches for lunch, and pink and black peppered salmon for dinner. These and a dozen more selections are either hot and spicy themselves, or are served with salsas, vinaigrettes, and marinades to increase their heat level.

2 pounds prawns, peeled and deveined	½ cup lime juice
¼ cup olive oil	8 cloves garlic, minced
2 ancho chiles, stems and seeds removed, softened in hot water, and finely minced	salt and pepper to taste
	¾ pound butter, cubed and cold
½ cup tequila	cilantro sprigs for garnish

Sauté the prawns in the olive oil until rare, then remove. Place everything else except the prawns, butter, and cilantro in the pan and reduce to ¼ volume. Slowly whisk in the butter over low heat, replace the prawns, and cook for one minute. Remove to plates, garnish with cilantro leaves, and serve with a fancy salad (see chapter 3).

Serves: 4
Heat Scale: Mild

CHIPOTLE SHRIMP WITH CORN CAKES
Coyote Café, Santa Fe, New Mexico

Mark Miller, executive chef and owner of the Coyote Café, is also the author of the bestselling cookbook of the same name, *Coyote Café* (Ten Speed Press, 1989), which is loaded with exotic chile pepper recipes. "I

like chipotles because of their smokiness and heat," says Mark of this recipe. "People love smoky food and smoke and chiles are a great combination."

CORN CAKES

¾ cup all-purpose flour
½ cup coarse corn meal
½ teaspoon baking powder
½ teaspoon baking soda
1 teaspoon salt
1 teaspoon sugar

1-¼ cups buttermilk
2 Tablespoons melted butter
1 egg, beaten
1 cup fresh corn kernels
2 green onions, chopped

Place the dry ingredients in a bowl and mix together. In a large bowl,
whisk the buttermilk and butter together and then whisk in the egg.
Gradually add the dry ingredients to the liquid and whisk until
thoroughly incorporated.

Puree ½ cup of the corn and fold it into the batter along with the remaining whole kernels and green onions. Add a little buttermilk, if
necessary, to thin the mixture.

Using a nonstick pan over medium heat, ladle the corn cake batter
into the pan and form 3-inch cakes. Cook until golden brown, about 2-½
minutes each side. Repeat with the remaining batter.

Yield: 18 to 20 cakes

CHIPOTLE SHRIMP

1-½ pounds medium shrimp,
    peeled, deveined, tails
    removed (about 30)
3 Tablespoons butter
1 cup softened butter
4-½ **Tablespoons canned
    chipotle chiles,** pureed

18 Corn Cakes
2 green onions, chopped
1 **cup fresh pico de gallo–
    type salsa** (see recipes,
    chapter 3)

Cook the shrimp in 3 tablespoons butter over low heat for about 5 minutes, turning them once.

Puree together the softened butter and the pureed chipotles and set
aside at room temperature.

Place 3 corn cakes on each plate, place 5 shrimp on top of the cakes, and spread the chipotle butter liberally over the shrimp. Sprinkle the chopped green onions over the shrimp and serve the salsa on the side.

Serves: 6
Heat Scale: Hot

〰〰〰〰〰〰〰

GRILLED SWORDFISH WITH A MANGO-HABANERO SALSA
La Tour Restaurant, Park Hyatt Hotel, Chicago, Illinois

Charles Weber, executive chef at the Park Hyatt, first experienced chiles when working with Mexican cooks in San Francisco. "They were into making 'killer' salsas—they wanted to burn me out!" he relates. "Before you knew it, I was enjoying the heat and the subtle flavors that chiles provide." He grows several varieties of Habanero chiles, so that his clientele can experience the exotic taste of the hottest chile in the world. "I love them," he confesses, "but they need to be respected as they can be dangerous."

3 large, ripe mangoes
1 lime
  red Habanero chiles (¼ chile for mild, 1 for medium, 2 for hot, and 3 for extremely hot), minced (serranos or jalapeños may be substituted in 3 to 1 quantities)

1 large bunch fresh cilantro, chopped fine
4 swordfish steaks
4 cloves garlic, crushed
  freshly cracked black pepper

Peel the mangoes, cut the meat away from the pits, and dice into ¼-inch pieces. Zest the lime and squeeze the juice from ½ of it. Combine the zest, juice, mangoes, Habaneros, and ½ of the cilantro and let this salsa sit for several hours before use.

Rub the swordfish steaks with a mixture of the rest of the cilantro, garlic, and cracked black pepper while the salsa is sitting. Grill the steaks over your favorite wood (mesquite, cherry, hickory) until done. Serve the steaks covered with the salsa.

Serves: 4

Heat Scale: Varies from Mild to Extremely Hot

~~~~~~~~~~~~~~~~

IXTAPA-STYLE RED SNAPPER WITH MARGARITA JALAPEÑO SALSA
Pecos River Café, New York, New York

Cookbook author and chef Jane Butel also owns her own chile and spice company, so she is a respected authority on hot and spicy foods. At the Pecos River Café, she puts into practice her own approach to good cooking: "I use spices to create fresh, clear flavors but not to overly complicate dishes." She uses all fresh ingredients, and all foods are prepared on the premises.

MARGARITA JALAPEÑO SALSA

4 or more fresh jalapeño chiles, very finely minced

½ cup cubed tomato (½-inch cubes)

½ cup medium-fine chopped red onion

1 clove garlic, minced

½ teaspoon salt (or to taste)

¼ cup gold or white tequila

Combine all ingredients and let stand for at least thirty minutes at room temperature. Taste and adjust seasonings.

Yield: 1-¼ cups

THE SNAPPER

½ cup all-purpose flour
½ teaspoon salt
   freshly ground black pepper
    to taste

¼ cup unsalted butter (or more,
   as needed)
6 six- to eight-ounce red snapper
   fillets

Combine the flour, salt, and pepper in a shallow, flat-bottomed dish. Melt the butter in a skillet. Dip the fillets in the flour mixture and cook in the butter, turning once, about five minutes per side or until they are a light, golden brown.

    Top the fillets with the salsa and place in the oven until the salsa is warmed. Serve the fillets on warmed plates, accompanied by rice.

Serves: 6
Heat Scale: Medium

SHRIMP RELLENOS
Calypso Caribbean Cuisine, Houston, Texas

Calypso is a re-creation of a Caribbean beachside bar, complete with large, saltwater aquariums as centerpieces and a kitchen behind a glass wall, so that customers can view the cooking process. "What makes Calypso different from most other Caribbean restaurants," says owner and chef Tim McGann, "is that we feature resort-style food rather than soul food." The emphasis is on spicy seafood, as this recipe indicates.

½   **teaspoon minced Scotch bonnet (Habanero) chiles,** stems removed and seeded
¼   pound butter
½   ounce anchovy paste
4   Tablespoons bread crumbs
25 large shrimp, peeled, cleaned, and deveined

1   beer
1-½ cups flour
1-½ Tablespoons ground ginger
1-½ Tablespoons salt
1-½ Tablespoons white pepper
1-½ Tablespoons baking powder
      vegetable oil for frying

Combine the first four ingredients and mix well. Make a cut ¾ of the way through the backs of the shrimp and stuff some of the mixture into each one.

Combine the remaining ingredients except the oil to make a batter. Dip each shrimp into the batter and fry in oil at 350 degrees until golden brown.

Serves: 4 to 6
Heat Scale: Medium

〰〰〰〰〰〰〰〰

CAJUN KITCHEN SINK PASTA WITH HOT ANDOUILLE SAUCE

Panama Red's Beach Bar and Seafood Grille, Nashville, Tennessee

Chef George Frezzell was born in Nashville, grew up in Baton Rouge, went to Louisiana State University on a basketball scholarship, attended the Culinary Institute of America, and then returned to Nashville to cook hot and spicy Cajun specialties at Panama Red's. His pasta creation below is Fettuccine Alfredo out of control!

ANDOUILLE SAUCE

¼ cup diced onions
⅛ cup diced red bell peppers
⅛ cup diced green bell peppers
12 ounces Andouille sausage, diced
½ stick unsalted butter
1 teaspoon cayenne powder
2 Tablespoons hot sauce such as Tabasco

¼ **cup Cajun seasoning such as Cajun Magic**
1 Tablespoon Worcestershire sauce
4 cups crushed fresh tomatoes
¼ cup tomato paste
2 Tablespoons dry red wine

Sauté the onions, peppers, and sausage in the butter. When the onions are translucent, add the remaining ingredients. Simmer for 10 minutes over medium heat.

Yield: 5 cups
Heat Scale: Hot

KITCHEN SINK PASTA

8 ounces your favorite white fish
8 ounces medium raw shrimp, peeled, deveined, and tails removed
8 ounces bay scallops, cleaned
8 ounces fresh shucked oysters

⅓ cup unsalted butter
6 Tablespoons dry white wine
2 pounds cooked fettuccine
½ cup heavy whipping cream
1-½ cups Andouille Sauce grated Parmesan cheese

Sauté the first four ingredients in the butter and wine for about 4 minutes. Add the fettuccine and cream and simmer for another 4 minutes. Add 1-½ cups (or more if necessary) of the Andouille Sauce and simmer until well thickened.

Top with the cheese and serve with a tossed green salad.

Serves: 4
Heat Scale: Medium

SEAFOOD COLORADO
La Cazuela, Northampton, Massachusetts

"Earthy brilliance" is a phrase chef Roe Schmidt uses to describe chiles and their many adaptations. She comments: "Some chiles are called on for their subtle earthiness and light sparkle on the tongue, while others are used for the bold fire they ignite in the senses. Chiles appeal to the soul as well as the tongue; they delight the eye as well as the palette and hold mystery as well as nutrition." The word "colorado" in this dish refers to a Spanish word indicating "red," rather than to the western state of the same name.

COLORADO SAUCE WITH DRIED CHIPOTLES

8 **dried chipotles,** stems and seeds removed

1 **Tablespoon ground red chile** (Hatch preferred)

1 teaspoon oregano

1 teaspoon salt

1 teaspoon cumin

1-½ cups minced onions

4 teaspoons minced garlic

2 Tablespoons olive oil

2 cups crushed tomatoes

1 cup shrimp broth (or substitute water)

Soak the chipotles in 1 cup of water for 2 hours. Place the chipotles and the soaking water in a blender and puree with the ground chile and the spices.

Sauté the onions and garlic in the oil over medium heat until they are soft. Add the pureed chipotles, tomatoes, and shrimp broth and simmer for about 15 minutes.

Yield: 5 cups
Heat Scale: Medium

THE SEAFOOD

2 Tablespoons olive oil

1 Tablespoon minced garlic

1 Tablespoon chopped cilantro

16 large shrimp, peeled and deveined

16 large sea scallops, muscles removed

2 cups Colorado Sauce

Heat the oil over medium heat and sauté the garlic and cilantro for about a minute. Add the seafood and sauté for about 5 minutes, until the shrimp turns pink and the scallops become opaque. Add 2 cups of Colorado Sauce and heat through. Serve over rice.

Serves: 4
Heat Scale: Medium

〰〰〰〰〰〰〰

ESCALOPE OF SALMON WITH CAPERS AND POBLANOS
The Rattlesnake Club, Detroit, Michigan

Jimmy Schmidt, executive chef and owner of The Rattlesnake Club, received much of his culinary training in France. He has received many honors for his creativity, including selection as a top chef by *Food and Wine, Cook's,* and *Master Chef* magazines. His Rattlesnake Club menus, which are rewritten every day, feature fresh local ingredients in season, rather than out-of-season exotica. As this recipe shows, Jimmy has been influenced by the rise of chile peppers in new American cuisine.

- **1 Tablespoon red New Mexican chile powder**
- 1 Tablespoon ground cumin
- ¼ cup cold water
- 1 cup safflower or corn oil
- 1 Tablespoon extra strong mustard
- ¼ cup lemon juice
- **1 Tablespoon chipotle chiles in adobo sauce,** minced
- salt and freshly ground black pepper to taste
- ½ cup dry white wine
- 1 Tablespoon virgin olive oil
- 8 escalopes of salmon, 3 ounces each
- ¼ cup nonpareil capers, drained
- **2 poblano chiles,** stems removed, roasted, peeled, seeded, and diced
- 1 Tablespoon toasted mustard seeds
- 4 sprigs fresh cilantro

In a small saucepan, combine the chile powder and cumin and moisten with ¼ cup of cold water. Add the safflower oil and, over medium heat, warm the oil to 160 degrees. Remove from the heat and pour into a tempered glass container. Refrigerate overnight. The next day, carefully pour the oil out of the jar and into a glass measuring cup, taking care that the spices remain in the jar.

In a blender, combine the mustard and the lemon juice. Slowly add the seasoned oil tablespoon by tablespoon until smooth and creamy. Add the chipotle chiles, blend, and adjust the salt and pepper to taste. Add the white wine to thin to sauce consistency. Reserve until ready to serve.

Brush the salmon escalopes with the olive oil and grill or broil them until well seared, about 2 minutes. Turn them over and cook to medium-rare, about 4 minutes.

Place 2 escalopes on each serving plate and pour the sauce over them in a band. Sprinkle the capers, poblanos, and mustard seeds over the sauce and garnish with the cilantro sprigs.

Serves: 4
Heat Scale: Mild

∿∿∿∿∿∿∿∿∿∿∿∿

JALAPEÑO-SMOKED SHRIMP WITH TAMALE SPOON-BREAD STICKS AND PINTO BEAN "RANCHERO" SAUCE
The Mansion on Turtle Creek, Dallas, Texas

This restaurant is undoubtedly the most elegant in Dallas. In 1925, cotton baron Sheppard W. King built this Italianate mansion, which was restored with a hotel addition in 1979 at a cost of $21 million. The restored mansion is now executive chef Dean Fearing's magnificent restaurant. Chef Fearing says of this recipe: "Once you have tried it, you will probably never eat a plain shrimp dish again."

TAMALE SPOON-BREAD STICKS

2 cups milk
1 cup masa harina
¼ cup yellow cornmeal
2 Tablespoons vegetable oil
½ large onion, sliced
1 teaspoon chopped garlic
¼ cup diced red bell pepper, seeded
1 **jalapeño chile,** stem removed, seeded, and chopped
2 **Tablespoons New Mexican green chile,** stem removed, roasted, peeled, seeded, and chopped
¼ pound cooked, ground chorizo sausage
¼ cup unsalted butter, softened
4 large eggs
1 teaspoon baking powder
¼ cup grated cheddar cheese
¼ **cup grated jalapeño jack cheese**
salt to taste

Bring the milk to a boil in a saucepan and then remove from the heat. Place the masa harina in a blender and, on a low setting, pour in half the hot milk and process until thoroughly blended. Add this mixture to the remaining hot milk in the saucepan and return to medium heat. Whisk in the cornmeal, whisking continuously to keep the masa from sticking. Lower the heat and simmer, stirring constantly, for 5 minutes. Remove from the heat.

Heat the oil in a sauté pan over medium heat and add the onion, garlic, bell pepper, and chiles and sauté until tender. Add the vegetables to the masa mixture along with the cooked chorizo. Beat in the butter and cool to room temperature. When cool, beat in the eggs, baking powder, cheeses, and salt.

Butter two cornstick pans. Fill each section with the spoon-bread batter and bake for 20 minutes at 350 degrees or until the sticks are brown. If the sticks begin to get too brown, cover the pans with foil. Serve hot.

Yield: 8 sticks
Heat Scale: Medium

PINTO BEAN "RANCHERO" SAUCE

1 cup cleaned pinto beans
2 Tablespoons corn oil
1 medium onion, diced
1 stalk celery, diced
1 small green bell pepper, seeded and diced
3 cloves garlic, minced
1 serrano chile, stem removed, seeded, and minced
4 cups chicken stock
2 tomatoes, peeled, seeded, and diced
½ teaspoon ground cumin
½ teaspoon ground coriander
1 Tablespoon black peppercorns
½ bay leaf

1 small bunch fresh thyme
1 small bunch fresh oregano
1 poblano chile, stem removed, roasted, peeled, seeded, and diced
1 small red bell pepper, roasted, peeled, seeded, and diced
1 small yellow bell pepper, roasted, peeled, seeded, and diced
1 teaspoon fresh lime juice
1 teaspoon your favorite bottled hot sauce, or more to taste
salt to taste

Cover the beans with 8 cups of cold water and soak for 8 hours, changing the water twice. Rinse and drain well before using.

Heat the oil in a saucepan and, over medium-high heat, sauté the onion, celery, and bell pepper for 4 minutes. Add the garlic and serrano and sauté for 1 minute. Add the drained beans, chicken stock, and tomatoes. Tie the spices and herbs into a cheesecloth bag, add to the bean mixture, and bring to a boil. Reduce heat and simmer, stirring occasionally, for 1 hour or until the beans are soft and the sauce is thick.

Remove the cheesecloth bag. Stir in the roasted poblano and bell peppers, season with the lime juice, hot sauce, and salt and keep warm until ready to serve.

Serves: 4
Heat Scale: Medium

JALAPEÑO-SMOKED SHRIMP

24 large Gulf shrimp, peeled, deveined, tails left on

3 jalapeño chiles, stems removed, seeded, chopped fine

¼ **cup finely chopped pickled jalapeño chiles**

¼ **cup juice from the pickled jalapeños**

3 shallots, peeled and chopped fine

3 cloves garlic, peeled and chopped fine

2 Tablespoons finely chopped fresh cilantro

1 Tablespoon finely chopped fresh epazote

3 Tablespoons fresh lime juice

2 Tablespoons olive oil salt to taste

4 sprigs fresh cilantro for garnish

Combine the shrimp with the fresh and pickled jalapeños, jalapeño juice, shallots, garlic, cilantro, epazote, and lime juice. Marinate for at least 2 hours, turning occasionally. Remove and drain well.

Smoke the shrimp in a smoker on as low heat as possible for 15 minutes. The shrimp should still be raw.

Heat 1 tablespoon of the olive oil in a large sauté pan. Season half the shrimp with salt and sauté over medium-high heat for 6 minutes or until the shrimp are opaque. Remove the shrimp to a platter, keep warm, and repeat the process with the remaining shrimp.

To serve: Crisscross 2 Tamale Spoon-Bread Sticks at the 12 o'clock position on each of 4 hot serving plates. Ladle a small portion of Pinto Bean "Ranchero" Sauce at the 6 o'clock position, making sure not to cover the entire plate. Lay the shrimp, tails up, at the top of the sauce. Place a sprig of cilantro on each plate between the spoon bread and the shrimp. Serve immediately.

Serves: 4
Heat Scale: Medium

BAHAMIAN SOUSED GROUPER
Pier House Restaurant, Key West, Florida

The Pier House specializes in creative West Indian cuisine, so it should come as no surprise that their seafood will be hot and spicy. A principal ingredient in this recipe by executive chef Brent Holleman is the Scotch bonnet or Habanero chile pepper. In addition to its heat, the Scotch bonnet also has a unique, "fruity" aroma that many chefs adore.

1 cup safflower oil or clarified butter

10 Scotch bonnet (Habanero) chiles, stems removed, seeded, and minced

2 green bell peppers, seeded and chopped medium

2 yellow bell peppers, seeded and chopped medium

2 red bell peppers, seeded and chopped medium

1 yellow onion, peeled and chopped medium

1 Tablespoon garlic, minced

1 Tablespoon shallots, minced

1 teaspoon mace

1 teaspoon ground coriander

1 teaspoon allspice

24 ounces fresh grouper, cut into 1-inch cubes

1 cup Key lime juice, freshly squeezed preferred

4 cups fish stock

2 tomatoes, peeled and chopped medium

¼ pound fresh spinach leaves

Heat the oil in a large skillet, add the chiles, bell peppers, onion, garlic, shallots, and spices and sauté for 3 to 5 minutes. Add the fish, lime juice, and fish stock and simmer for 6 to 8 minutes. Taste and add salt if necessary. Add the tomatoes and simmer gently until they are soft, about 3 minutes.

To serve, line a large soup plate with spinach leaves and pour in the soused fish.

Serves: 4
Heat Scale: Hot

PAN-FRIED "CRISP" RED SNAPPER ON A SIZZLING PLATTER
Claire Restaurant, New York, New York

Claire restaurant chef, Dhanit Choladda, was born in a small fishing village in eastern Thailand and learned to cook in the "Thai tradition" of fresh ingredients, tantalizing spices, and flavors that "wake you up." He and the owner, Marvin Paige, personally select the fresh fish at the market several mornings a week. This snapper should be served very hot and accompanied by white rice with a cilantro garnish.

2   pounds fresh red snapper fillets, scaled but not skinned
    flour
    cooking oil for deep frying
6   jalapeños, stems removed, seeded, and chopped fine
1   clove garlic, minced

½   cup minced onion
1   Tablespoon butter
1   teaspoon chopped cilantro root
1   teaspoon sugar
2   teaspoons fish sauce
2   teaspoons vinegar
1   teaspoon lemon juice

Coat the fillets with flour and deep fry until brown and slighty crisp. Remove them, drain, and keep warm.

In a saucepan, sauté the jalapeños, garlic, and onion in the butter for about three minutes. Add the remaining ingredients and cook for another 5 minutes or until thickened.

Heat a platter in the oven until it is very hot. Place the fillets on it and pour the sauce over them.

Serves: 4
Heat Scale: Hot

TACOS DE PESCADO
La Paz Restaurante Mexicano, Atlanta, Georgia

La Paz owner/chef Tom Nickoloff has over fifteen years of experience cooking Southwestern foods, and this recipe is one of his favorites. In his spare time, he grows a variety of chiles on his farm in the north Georgia mountains. He explains his attitude toward hot and spicy foods as "just a craving."

6   ounces fresh swordfish or mahi-mahi steaks

¼ **cup New Mexican green chiles,** stems removed, roasted, peeled, seeded, and cut into strips

1 **serrano chile,** stem removed, seeded, and minced

¼ cup diced fresh tomatoes

¼ cup diced onion

½ cup fresh chopped cilantro

2 Tablespoons pepitas (pumpkin seeds)

3 Tablespoons butter

4 taco shells or fresh corn tortillas which have been softened by frying them in vegetable oil for a few seconds

lime wedges for garnish

Broil or charbroil the fish until medium done, then set aside.

Mix together the green chile strips, serranos, tomatoes, onions, and cilantro.

Sauté the pepitas in the butter for 1 minute. Add the pepper mixture and cook over medium heat for 2 more minutes. Cut the fish into ½-inch cubes, add to the pan, and cook 1 more minute, mashing the fish slightly.

Add the mixture to the taco shells, or wrap with the softened corn tortillas. Garnish with lime wedges and serve.

Serves: 4
Heat Scale: Medium

CHILE-WRAPPED SHRIMP WITH PINEAPPLE SALSA
Culinary Capers, Baltimore, Maryland

Chef Nona Nielsen-Parker caters to clients looking for something different—those with "adventuresome palates," as she puts it. When the restaurant she was working in burned down, she decided to start her own catering business. "I believe food should be fun and look as beautiful as it tastes," she says. By alternating red and green chiles as wrappings for the shrimp, a stunning effect is created with this recipe.

PINEAPPLE SALSA

1 **Tablespoon minced jalapeño,** stem and seeds removed

½ cup finely chopped fresh pineapple

½ teaspoon finely grated fresh ginger

1 plum tomato, seeded and minced

sprinkle of minced cilantro

Combine all ingredients and allow to sit for an hour to blend the flavors.

Yield: ¾ cup

CHILE-WRAPPED SHRIMP

4 **fresh New Mexican chiles** (2 green and 2 red if possible), stems removed, roasted, peeled, seeded, and cut into strips

24 large shrimp, peeled, deveined, tails removed

2 Tablespoons olive oil

Wrap each shrimp with a strip of chile, alternating red and green, tucking the seam under the bottom of the shrimp. Put the shrimps in an oiled baking dish. Drizzle a small amount of oil on each shrimp, place under the broiler, and broil until done, about 2 minutes.

Serve with the salsa on the side.

Serves: 3 to 4
Heat Scale: Mild

CAMARONES AL AJILLO
Zarela Restaurant, New York, New York

Restaurateur and caterer Zarela Martinez once bribed a waiter in a Mexico City restaurant with $100 to find the secret ingredient in this shrimp and garlic sauce creation. She discovered it was the powdered chicken stock that made the dish taste so good, so she cautions that this is one of the few recipes where the powdered concentrate yields better results than the fresh stock.

2	Tablespoons finely minced garlic	4	**fresh poblano chiles,** stems removed, roasted, peeled, and seeded
1	Tablespoon powdered chicken stock base	2	pounds large shrimp, deveined but left in shells
1-½	cups extra virgin olive oil		salt to taste
6	**dried New Mexican chiles,** stems removed, seeded		juice of one lime

In a small bowl, combine the garlic and chicken stock base with the olive oil and marinate overnight.

Cut the chiles crosswise into ¼-inch rings and marinate them in the oil and garlic mixture for 3 to 4 hours.

Remove half the chiles and garlic from the oil mixture and reserve. Heat the remaining oil with chiles and garlic in a deep skillet until it bubbles. Add half the shrimp and fry, turning once, until they turn pink, 2 to 3 minutes on each side. Remove the shrimp and other solids with a slotted spoon, drain, and keep warm. Add the remaining chiles and garlic to the oil and repeat the process with the remaining shrimp. Season the shrimp with salt and lime juice and serve immediately.

Serves: 6
Heat Scale: Medium

GET 'EM HOT SHRIMP PASTA
Mildred's VIP Catering, Jackson, Mississippi

Chefs all over the country are combining hot chiles with every imaginable ingredient. Mildred Brown's inventive combination includes shrimp, pasta, cream cheese, and sour cream. The last two ingredients will cut the heat of the jalapeños, so add more chiles if you want this dish to be hotter.

1 package of your favorite pasta	1 tomato, chopped fine
4 Tablespoons jalapeños, stems removed, seeded, chopped fine	2 pounds cooked shrimp, peeled and deveined
1 cup chopped green onions	2 8-ounce packages cream cheese
½ cup chopped bell pepper	½ cup sour cream
1 stick unsalted butter	

Boil the pasta until done, drain, sprinkle with olive oil, mix, and keep warm.

Sauté the chiles, onions, and bell pepper in the butter until soft. Add the tomatoes and shrimp and cook for 2 minutes.

Cut the cream cheese into four pieces, add to the skillet, and let melt. Add the sour cream at the last minute, heat through, and remove from the heat.

Toss the shrimp mixture with the pasta and serve immediately.

Serves: 4
Heat Scale: Medium

GRILLED GREAT LAKES WHITEFISH WITH POBLANO PEPPER PESTO

Too Chez, Novi, Michigan

Executive Chef Edward Janos is currently pursuing his Masters Chef Certification through the American Culinary Federation. The Too Chez, an eclectic establishment that was voted Best Restaurant of the Year 1991 in the Detroit area, serves seasonal foods from many different ethnic cuisines. It features products indigenous to the Great Lakes area, as this recipe indicates.

POBLANO PEPPER PESTO

1 **cup chopped poblano chiles,** roasted, peeled, stems removed, seeded, and chopped

2 cloves garlic, minced

1 cup piñon nuts

1 cup basil leaves

1 cup cilantro leaves

1 cup grated Parmesan-Reggiano cheese

1 **Tablespoon Inner Beauty hot sauce,** or other mustard-base hot sauce such as Matouk's, or mustard combined half and half with a hot sauce

1 cup olive oil

In a food processor, puree the first 7 ingredients. Drizzle in oil and mix lightly.

Yield: 2-½ cups
Heat Scale: Medium

GRILLED GREAT LAKES WHITEFISH

4 10-ounce boned whitefish fillets (or substitute other firm white fish)

1 Tablespoon red chile powder

4 cups new potatoes, boiled until done, quartered

3 cups green beans, blanched

1 cup mushrooms, quartered and blanched

salt and pepper to taste

½ cup fish stock

¼ cup dry white wine

2 cups onions, sliced and caramelized by sautéing in butter and a little sugar

1 cup Poblano Pepper Pesto

Sprinkle the whitefish with chile powder, salt, and pepper and grill until done. Remove from heat and keep warm.

Heat the fish stock and wine in a pan, add the potatoes and cook until heated. Add the green beans, mushrooms, and onions and cook over medium heat for 1 minute. Add the pesto and heat through.

Spoon the potato mixture onto a plate and top with the whitefish.

Serves: 4
Heat Scale: Medium

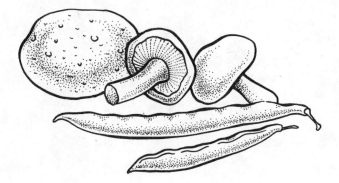

Pungent Poultry

I n 1825, Jean-Anthelme Brillat-Savarin wrote in his book, *The Philosopher in the Kitchen:* "Fowls are to the kitchen what the canvas is to the painter; they are served up to us boiled, roasted, fried, hot or cold, whole or in pieces, with or without sauce, boned, skinned, or stuffed, and always with equal success."

Poultry is still being served in all these ways, of course, but nowadays a wide variety of chile peppers is being combined with it, especially with chicken. Why? Because today's mass-produced chickens reach their optimum three-pound weight in just two months, and consequently the taste of their meat is rather bland. Many chefs are now using "free-range" chickens, which are allowed the freedom to run around in a yard rather than spending their entire lives in a cage. The flavor of the free-range chickens is reputedly tasty enough to justify prices two or three times what supermarket chickens command.

However, there are advantages to the mass-produced chickens. Aside from being relatively inexpensive, they are nutritious, easy to digest, and quick to prepare. As food expert Howard Hillman has noted, "Chicken marries well with most flavoring ingredients and its taste can be readily changed from semi-insipid to savory." One of the best ways to accomplish that is to combine chicken and chiles, as these recipes demonstrate.

ROAST CHICKEN WITH GREEN AND RED PIPIAN SAUCES
Coyote Café, Santa Fe, New Mexico

Before becoming one of this country's premiere chefs, Mark Miller studied anthropology at Berkeley, which explains his rather historical approach to food. He notes about this recipe: "Pumpkin seed or *pipian* sauces, which I think of as Southwestern pestos, date from pre-Columbian days. The conquistadors Cortez and Bernal Díaz recorded that *pipians* were served at some of Montezuma's court feasts. The flavors of red chiles thickened with pumpkin seed puree were also the basis for *mole* sauces." The hot red pipian sauce contrasts with the "cool" green pipian sauce in Mark's colorful recipe.

RED PIPIAN SAUCE

2   **whole dried ancho chiles,** stems removed, seeded
4   **whole dried red New Mexican chiles,** stems removed, seeded
1   quart water
¾   pound Roma tomatoes
½   cup finely chopped white onion
2   Tablespoons olive oil
4   ounces green unroasted pumpkin seeds (about 1 heaping cup)
6   cloves garlic, roasted
2   **canned chipotle chiles in adobo sauce**
1   **teaspoon adobo sauce**
½   cup dry roasted peanuts
½   teaspoon ground allspice
2   teaspoons canela (or 1 teaspoon cinnamon)
    pinch ground clove
1   teaspoon sugar
1-½   teaspoons salt
1   Tablespoon duck fat or peanut oil

With a comal or black iron skillet, or in an oven at 250 degrees, dry roast the ancho and New Mexican chiles for 5 minutes. Shake once or twice and do not allow to blacken. Add them to the water in a covered pan and simmer very low for 30 minutes to rehydrate. Allow to cool.

Blacken the tomatoes in a skillet or under a broiler (about 5 minutes). Sauté the onions in the oil over low heat until slightly browned.

Dry roast the pumpkin seeds in a sauté pan for about 5 minutes until they have finished popping. Place them in a blender and puree together with tomatoes to form a paste. Add the roasted chiles, about ½ cup of chile water if not bitter (or use plain water), and the remaining ingredients, except the duck fat, and puree further.

Add the duck fat to a high-sided pan and heat until almost smoking. Refry the sauce at a sizzle for 3 to 5 minutes, stirring constantly.

Yield: 5 cups

Heat Scale: Hot

GREEN PIPIAN SAUCE

4	ounces green untoasted pumpkin seeds (about 1 heaping cup)	1	bunch watercress
½	cup finely chopped white onion	1	bunch radish tops
		1-½	teaspoons roasted anise seed
2	Tablespoons peanut oil	1	teaspoon salt
1	cup rich chicken stock	1	teaspoon sugar
1-½	cups fresh cilantro	1	Tablespoon duck fat or peanut oil
2	cloves garlic, roasted		
8	large leaves romaine lettuce, chopped (no stems)		

Dry roast the pumpkin seeds in a sauté pan for about 5 minutes until they have finished popping. Set aside a few seeds for garnish. Sauté the onion in the oil over low heat until slightly browned. Place the seeds and stock in a blender and form a paste. Add ½ cup of the cilantro and the remaining ingredients except the fat, and puree.

Add the duck fat or oil to a high-sided pan and heat until almost smoking. Refry the sauce at a sizzle for 3 to 4 minutes, stirring continuously; do not overcook or the sauce will lose its greenness. Return to blender, add the remaining cup of cilantro, and puree together. Garnish with the reserved pumpkin seeds.

Yield: 4 cups

THE CHICKEN

2 chickens, preferably free-
   range, about 4 pounds each
2 teaspoons salt
2 **Tablespoons mild red chile
   powder**

½ cup Red Pipian Sauce
½ cup Green Pipian Sauce
   cilantro sprigs

Remove the backbones from the chickens and cut them in half. Season with a mixture of the salt and the chile powder. Roast them in a hot 450 degree oven for 15 minutes or until the juice runs clear when a knife is inserted.

Prepare the pipian sauces. Place ¼ cup of each on either side of 4 plates. Place the chicken on top of the sauce, and garnish with cilantro.

Serves: 4
Heat Scale: Varies

CHEESE AND HOT PEPPER CHICKEN
K-Paul's Louisiana Kitchen,
New Orleans, Louisiana

In an interview, K-Paul's famous chef, Paul Prudhomme, discussed how chile peppers entered his life: "In our house, Mother didn't cook with peppers, but we always had a variety of hot peppers on the table. Mother would put our cayenne peppers or bird's-eye peppers, which grow wild here in south Louisiana, in a vinegar. Or she would chop up other local peppers and make them into a sauce. Sometimes the sauce would have tomatoes in it and then it would taste sweet and hot all at once. These pepper mixtures would be on the table at all times, for every meal of the day, so we could always put heat into our food. This custom gave me the opportunity to taste the different kinds of peppers and see how they affected the flavors of a variety of foods." Chef Paul's spice mixtures are available by mail; see chapter 1.)

3	**Tablespoons Poultry Magic** or other Cajun spice blend
1	teaspoon dry mustard
½	teaspoon cumin
¼	teaspoon ground cinnamon
1-¼	cups all-purpose flour
2	chickens, 2-½ to 3 pounds each, cut into 16 pieces, and at room temperature
	cooking oil for frying
2-⅔	cups chopped green bell peppers
2	cups chopped onions
1	**cup chopped New Mexican green chiles,** roasted, peeled, seeded, stems removed
2	bay leaves

2	teaspoons salt
2	teaspoons minced garlic
¾	teaspoon white pepper
¾	teaspoon black pepper
1-½	**teaspoons cayenne powder**
2	**Tablespoons finely chopped jalapeños**
4	cups chicken stock
1-½	cups heavy cream
1	cup dairy sour cream
1-½	cups grated Monterey Jack cheese or other white (preferably nonprocessed) cheese
1-½	cups grated cheddar cheese
4	cups cooked rice

Thoroughly combine the Poultry Magic with the mustard, cumin, and cinnamon in a small bowl, breaking up any mustard lumps. Combine 1 tablespoon of this mixture with the flour in a plastic or paper bag and set aside. Remove any excess fat from chicken pieces.

Sprinkle the remaining seasoning mixture evenly on the chicken, patting it in by hand. Dredge the chicken in the seasoned flour and reserve the leftover flour.

Heat ½-inch of oil in a large skillet (this dish tastes significantly better if you *don't* use a nonstick skillet) to 350 degrees. Fry the chicken in batches, large pieces first, skin side down, just until light brown and crispy, about 2 to 4 minutes per side. (Lower the heat if drippings in the pan start to brown; you will use the drippings in the cream sauce, and you need them to remain light in color and taste so they won't dominate the cheese, peppers, and cream flavors.) Drain on paper towels.

Carefully pour the hot oil into a glass measuring cup, leaving as much sediment as possible in the skillet. Return ½ cup hot oil to the skillet. Add 2 cups of the bell peppers, the onions, and ⅔ cup of the green chiles; turn heat to high and scrape and stir well to mix vegetables with the sediment on the pan bottom.

Cook until onions start to brown, about 6 to 8 minutes, stirring occasionally. Add the bay leaves, salt, garlic, and the white, black, and red (cayenne) peppers; stir well. Then sprinkle 3 tablespoons of the reserved flour on the vegetable mixture and stir thoroughly. Stir in the jalapeños and cook about 2 minutes, stirring occasionally (lower heat if sticking excessively). Stir in 1 cup of the stock and scrape the pan bottom well. Add 2 more cups of stock and stir. Remove from heat. Place the chicken in a 5-½ quart saucepan or large Dutch oven.

Add the vegetable mixture and the remaining 1 cup stock to the chicken and stir well. Bring to a boil, then simmer over low heat for 15 minutes, stirring occasionally and being careful not to let the mixture scorch. Add the remaining ⅔ cup bell peppers, ⅓ cup green chiles, the cream, and sour cream. Bring to a boil over medium heat, stirring fairly constantly. Then stir in the cheeses and cook just until cheese melts, stirring constantly.

Serve immediately, allowing about ½ cup rice and 2 pieces of chicken per serving, topped with about ⅔ cup sauce. (Leftover sauce is wonderful over vegetables.)

Serves: 8
Heat Scale: Medium

THE LOON CHICKEN CHIMICHANGA
The Loon Café, Minneapolis, Minnesota

The Loon, which specializes in chili con carne, also serves other Southwestern specialties, including chimichangas. No one knows the origin of this word, which translates as "thing-a-ma-jig." It is, basically, a deep-fried burrito. Chef and manager of The Loon, Jeff Johnson, is of Swedish ancestry but says he has fallen in love with hot and spicy food, particularly New Mexican and Sichuan cuisines.

1	green bell pepper, julienned	**1**	**Tablespoon New Mexican red chile powder**
1	red bell pepper, julienned		
1	**jalapeño,** stem removed, seeded, and minced	1	Tablespoon ground cumin
1	medium onion, peeled and chopped fine	1	teaspoon onion powder
		2	teaspoons black pepper
1-½	pounds of cooked chicken, chopped	6	12-inch flour tortillas
			corn oil for deep frying
			shredded lettuce

In a skillet sauté the bell peppers, the jalapeño, and the onion in a little oil until soft. Add the remaining ingredients except the tortillas, oil, and lettuce and simmer for 5 minutes. Remove the mixture from the heat and cool.

Divide the mixture into 6 equal parts and place each part in the center of a tortilla. Fold in the sides and secure them with a toothpick or wooden skewer.

Deep fry each chimichanga in corn oil at 375 degrees for five minutes or until golden brown.

Serve the chimichangas on a bed of shredded letture topped with a sauce selected from chapter 3, and sour cream if desired.

Serves: 6
Heat Scale: Mild

FOUR-PEPPER GARLIC CHICKEN
Panama Red's Beach Bar and Seafood Grille, Nashville, Tennessee

This restaurant, a favorite of Nashville's Music Row and among musicians such as John Denver, Steve Winwood, and the members of Alabama, is described by owner John Cowan as "a mixture of coastal and Cajun cuisine with a heavy Caribbean influence." This recipe was developed by chef Ed Arace, who comments: "I couldn't cook without peppers or hot sauce—even in my delicate dishes a little dash of sauce or a small amount of peppers will enhance it without overpowering it." This poultry dish, however, is not among the delicate.

¼ cup diced onion	2 Tablespoons soy sauce
¼ cup diced green bell pepper	1-½ pounds boned and skinned chicken breasts, cut into 1-inch squares
¼ cup diced red bell pepper	
¼ cup diced celery	flour for dredging
4 cloves garlic, minced	1 cup chicken stock
¼ cup sliced mushrooms	1 teaspoon sugar
1 Tablespoon peeled and minced fresh ginger	juice of 1 lime
2 Scotch bonnet (Habanero) chiles, stems removed, seeded, and finely minced	2 teaspoons cornstarch
	2 teaspoons cooking sherry
	3 cups cooked wild or white rice
1 cup olive oil	¼ cup sliced green onions for garnish
1 fresh cayenne chile (or other hot variety), stem removed, seeded, and finely minced	

Sauté the onion, bell peppers, celery, garlic, mushrooms, ginger, and Scotch bonnet in ¼ cup of the oil for about 3 minutes. Add the cayenne and the soy sauce and cook for 2 minutes more.

Roll the chicken pieces in flour and, in another pan, fry them in the remaining oil until brown, about 5 minutes. Drain the pieces on paper towels and keep warm.

To the sautéed vegetables, add the chicken stock, sugar, and lime juice and bring to a boil. Add the cornstarch to the sherry, mix well, and add it to the vegetables, continuing to cook over medium heat. Add the chicken and stir constantly until thickened.

Divide the rice equally among 4 plates, serve the chicken around it, and garnish with the green onions.

Serves: 4
Heat Scale: Hot

HOT ORANGE CHICKEN
The Riverwood, Boone, North Carolina

A restaurant for over thirty years, The Riverwood building obviously has longevity. The owners, Randy Plachy and Sara Littlejohn, enjoy their work and have a good time while making the food taste and look good. "We take our food seriously without taking ourselves too seriously," they say. This fiery chicken recipe takes its heat from a unique orange sauce that gets hotter and hotter as it sits in the refrigerator.

HOT ORANGE SAUCE

1 **fistful dried piquin chiles,** or substitute other small dried red chiles such as "Chinese," santaka, chile de árbol, or cayenne

½ **Tablespoon chile oil**

1 teaspoon orange extract

1 Tablespoon minced garlic

1 Tablespoon brandy

½ cup orange marmalade

½ Tablespoon tamari

1 teaspoon black pepper

zest of 3 oranges

juice of 8 oranges

2 cups water

¼ cup cornstarch

Combine all ingredients except the water and cornstarch and let the mixture sit for at least 24 hours. Do not blend in a blender. Dissolve the cornstarch in the water and add to the other ingredients. Keep refrigerated, and it will last about a month.

Yield: 1 quart
Heat Scale: Hot

THE CHICKEN

2 8-ounce chicken breasts

½ cup red onion cut into strips

½ cup red bell pepper cut into strips

¼ cup sliced scallions

2 Tablespoons thinly sliced red cabbage

¼ cup sliced carrot

1 cup Hot Orange Sauce

Place all ingredients in a sauté pan and heat over medium-high heat until the chicken is done, about 15 minutes. Add more sauce if necessary. Serve over rice pilaf.

Serves: 2
Heat Scale: Medium

~~~~~~~~~~~~

POLLO ASADO DEL PUEBLO WITH JUNIPER BERRIES AND TWO SAUCES
La Cazuela, Northampton, Massachusetts

La Cazuela co-owners, Roe Schmidt and Barry Steeves, have had to triumph over the adversity of "New Englanders suspicious of Mexican food," and they have succeeded because of their contemporary variations on traditional ingredients and techniques. Chef Schmidt believes that the food served in her restaurant should be as good as if it were prepared at home for just a few guests. This interesting grilled chicken recipe offers the diner the choice of two sauces, but many customers use both!

CHIPOTLE-PIQUIN SAUCE

1-½	cups piquin chiles	1	teaspoon cumin
2	Tablespoons chipotle seeds	¼	cup red wine vinegar
1	Tablespoon black pepper	1	cup water

Process all ingredients in a blender until smooth. For best flavor, refrigerate for 3 days before using.

Yield: 1-½ cups
Heat Scale: Extremely Hot

HATCH CHILE SAUCE

2　Tablespoons flour
3　Tablespoons mixed olive oil
　　and corn oil
½　**cup ground red New Mexican chile** (Hatch preferred)

2　cups chicken broth
½　cup tomato sauce
2　teaspoons oregano leaf
1　teaspoon minced garlic
½　teaspoon ground cumin

Brown the flour in the oil over medium heat for about 3 minutes. Add the ground chile and continue browning, stirring constantly. Add the chicken broth, whisking constantly to avoid lumping. Add the remaining ingredients and simmer for 15 minutes.

Yield: 3 cups
Heat Scale: Medium

POLLO ASADO

3　Tablespoons juniper berries
¼　**cup ground red Dixon chile** (hot red chile)
2　**Tablespoons ground red Hatch chile** (mild chile)

¼　cup lime juice
12　half chicken breasts, 3 ounces each
　　Hatch Chile Sauce
　　Chipotle-Piquin Sauce

Roast the juniper berries in a skillet over high heat for about 5 minutes, shaking constantly. Let cool, then grind in a mortar until fine.

Mix 2 tablespoons of the ground juniper berries with the ground chiles and add the lime juice a little at a time until the mixture is the consistency of a runny paste. Add the chicken breasts, coat thoroughly, and marinate overnight in a glass bowl.

Grill the breasts for about 4 minutes a side over medium-hot coals. Ladle about ⅓ cup of the Hatch Chile Sauce over 2 breasts and sprinkle with ½ teaspoon of the ground juniper berries. Serve with a side of the Chipotle-Piquin Sauce to increase the heat level.

Serves: 6
Heat Scale: Medium to Hot

JALAPEÑO-SMOKED CHICKEN FAJITA WITH GRILLED ONION GUACAMOLE AND WATERMELON PICO DE GALLO

The Mansion on Turtle Creek, Dallas, Texas

Executive chef Dean Fearing is one of the nation's foremost proponents of "New Southwest" cuisine, which combines fresh, local ingredients with classic culinary methods. He is the author of *Dean Fearing's Southwest Cuisine* (Grove Weidenfeld, 1990), from which this recipe is adapted. He credits the origin of this recipe to Chef Jody Denton, but says he had to decipher it.

GRILLED ONION GUACAMOLE

2 Tablespoons corn oil

2 Tablespoons fresh lemon juice

1 Tablespoon red wine vinegar

1 teaspoon crushed black pepper

1 teaspoon ground whole cumin seeds

¾ teaspoon salt

1 large red onion, sliced ¼-inch thick

3 ripe avocados, peeled, pitted, and diced

1 large tomato, diced

3 **serrano chiles,** stems removed, seeded, and chopped

2 cloves garlic, minced

1 small bunch fresh cilantro, chopped

2 teaspoons fresh lime juice

Combine the first six ingredients for a marinade and mix well. Add the onion slices and marinate for 1 hour. Drain off the marinade and grill the onion slices on a hot grill for 3 minutes per side. Mix the slices with the remaining ingredients and keep at room temperature until ready for use.

Yield: 2 cups

Heat Scale: Medium

WATERMELON PICO DE GALLO

1   **jalapeño chile,** stem removed, seeded, and chopped

½   cup diced jicama

1-½   cups watermelon, diced ¼-inch, seeds removed

¼   cup honeydew melon, diced ¼-inch, seeds removed

¼   cup cantaloupe, diced ¼-inch, seeds removed

¼   cup red onion, diced ¼-inch

2   Tablespoons fresh lime juice

½   cup chopped fresh cilantro leaves

salt to taste

Combine all ingredients just before serving and mix lightly so as not to break up the watermelon.

Yield: 3 cups
Heat Scale: Mild

CHICKEN FAJITAS

4   boned, skinned chicken breasts

3   **jalapeño chiles,** stems removed, 2 seeded, all minced

⅛   **teaspoon ground cayenne**

1   large onion, sliced

2   shallots, chopped

1   small bunch cilantro, chopped

1-½   teaspoons crushed black pepper

1-½   cups dark beer

½   cup corn oil

8   warm flour tortillas

Combine the chicken breasts and the other ingredients except the tortillas and marinate for 2 hours at room temperature.

Prepare the smoker, remove the breasts from the marinade, and smoke, using as little heat as possible for 15 to 20 minutes. Return the breasts to the marinade for another hour.

Prepare a grill and make sure the grate is clean and oiled. Remove the chicken from the marinade and grill on one side for 4 minutes. Turn and grill the other side for 3 minutes. When done, cut the breasts into thin strips.

Serve the chicken with flour tortillas, the Grilled Onion Guacamole, and the Watermelon Pico de Gallo. Guests may roll the chicken with the two sauces in the tortillas.

Serves: 4
Heat Scale: Medium

wwwwwwwwww

GALANTINE OF ROAST QUAIL WITH BLUE CORN DRESSING AND BLACKBERRY CHIPOTLE SAUCE
La Casa Sena, Santa Fe, New Mexico

The *Santa Fe New Mexican* described La Casa Sena as showing "luminescent signs of star quality," and to chef Kip McClerin that means a dedication to native heritage, local produce (in some recipes, he uses as many as twelve different varieties of chile peppers), and constant innovation. This recipe combines pre-Columbian game, French technique, and Native American blue corn and chiles.

BLACKBERRY CHIPOTLE SAUCE

2 Tablespoons butter	1 cup fresh blackberries
3 Tablespoons flour	¼ cup blackberry brandy
3 chipotle chiles, rehydrated, stems removed, minced (or substitute chipotles in adobo sauce, minced)	1 cup red wine
	2 cups chicken stock
	pinch nutmeg

Make a roux with the butter and flour. Simmer the other ingredients in a saucepan for 2 minutes, add the roux, and simmer on low heat for 30 minutes, or until thickened.

Yield: 2 cups

BLUE CORN DRESSING

½ cup heavy cream
1 egg yolk
¼ cup chopped scallions, white part only
¼ **cup chopped New Mexican green chile**
¼ cup chopped cilantro
¼ cup chopped fresh rosemary, leaves only
2 Tablespoons butter
4 blue corn muffins, crumbled
¼ cup grated Monterey Jack cheese

Whisk the cream and the egg yolk together and set aside. Sauté the scallions, chiles, cilantro, and rosemary in the butter for a couple of minutes, then add the muffins. Continue to cook for 1 minute and then add the cream and yolk mixture. Remove from the heat, stir, add the cheese, and blend thoroughly.

Cool to room temperature.

THE QUAILS

8 quails
  walnut oil
  fresh rosemary, stemmed and chopped
  salt and cracked black pepper to taste
Blue Corn Dressing
Blackberry Chipotle Sauce

Partially bone the quails by removing the back and breast bone (this is known as "European boned"). Rub the birds with walnut oil and season inside and outside with the rosemary, salt, and pepper. Stuff the cavities with the blue corn dressing.

Arrange them in a baking dish breasts up and roast for about 20 minutes in a 350 degree oven, or until the skin is well browned.

Serve 2 quails to a plate with the sauce served over them.

Serves: 4
Heat Scale: Medium

GRILLED CHICKEN WITH BLACK PEPPER AND CILANTRO
Culinary Capers, Baltimore, Maryland

Caterer Nona Nielsen-Parker was taught as a child to try any and all foods at least once, which gave her an open mind and a desire to experiment with different combinations of ingredients. She believes that chiles should be an accent but should not dominate the taste of the food.

CILANTRO MARINADE

½ teaspoon chile paste with garlic
2 large garlic cloves, crushed
1 teaspoon brown sugar

1 Tablespoon fish sauce
2 Tablespoons peanut oil
¼ cup finely chopped cilantro

Combine all the ingredients.

Yield: ¼ cup

THE DIPPING SAUCE

½ teaspoon chile paste with garlic
5 Tablespoons fish sauce
3 Tablespoons rice vinegar

2 Tablespoons freshly squeezed lime juice
2 Tablespoons brown sugar

Combine all ingredients.

Yield: ¾ cup

THE CHICKEN

1 pound chicken breasts, boned, skinned, and cut into 1-inch cubes
2 teaspoons coarsely ground black pepper

Cilantro Marinade
Dipping Sauce

Toss the chicken in the pepper, place it in a bowl, and cover with the marinade. Refrigerate and marinate overnight.

Thread the chicken on wooden skewers which have been soaked in water. Grill over medium coals until done, approximately 10 minutes. Serve with the Dipping Sauce.

Serves: 2
Heat Scale: Medium

〰〰〰〰〰〰〰

TAMALE-STUFFED GAME HENS
Majestic Diner, Austin, Texas

The art deco Majestic is a contemporary diner designed to resemble a classic one of the '30s and '40s. The regular menu features comfort foods such as chicken fried steak, pot roast, and chicken and dumplings, but on the daily specials, chef Mick Vann goes crazy with hot and spicy creations from the Southwest, the Caribbean, and Southeast Asia.

2 Tablespoons hot red New Mexican chile powder	2 cups grated Monterey Jack cheese
¼ cup chopped onion	¼ bunch green onions, minced fine
2 Tablespoons garlic in oil	1 teaspoon granulated garlic
3 cups tomato juice	1 teaspoon cumin
1 Tablespoon cumin	1 teaspoon oregano
1 Tablespoon oregano	**1 teaspoon hot chile powder**
2 bay leaves	**2 cups tomatillo or red chile sauce** (see recipes, chapter 3)
½ cup olive oil	
3 game hens, rinsed and cleaned	
6 tamales	

Combine the first 8 ingredients and mix well. Marinate the hens in the mixture for at least 4 hours and preferably overnight.

Steam the tamales for 25 minutes, then remove them from the wrappers and crumble them. Add the remaining ingredients except sauce and mix well.

Stuff the hens and roast them for an hour at 325 degrees, or until they are crispy. Remove the hens from the oven and carefully cut them in half lengthwise, taking care to keep the stuffing in the cavity. Serve stuffing side up and top with a tomatillo or red chile sauce.

Serves: 6
Heat Scale: Medium

~~~~~~~~~~~~~~~~~~~~~~~~

GINGERED CHICKEN WITH MANGO
Calypso Caribbean Cuisine, Houston, Texas

At Calypso, the origin of each dish on the menu is listed with its description. Jamaica appears often, of course, but other islands of interest include Haiti, Cuba, Martinique, Aruba, and the home of the recipe below, Guadeloupe.

4 8-ounce chicken breasts, boned and skinned
vegetable oil for frying
¼ cup dark brown sugar
¼ teaspoon freshly ground cloves
2 Tablespoons peeled, minced ginger

¼ **teaspoon minced Scotch bonnet (Habanero) chiles,** stems removed and seeded (or more to taste)
½ teaspoon soy sauce
1 cup peeled and diced mangoes

Sauté the chicken breasts in a little oil until browned. Remove from the skillet and keep warm. Wipe the skillet clean, add 1 teaspoon of oil and all the other ingredients except the mangoes. Cook until thick and bubbly. Add the mangoes and cook until warm. Place the chicken back into the mixture and heat gently. Serve with rice.

Serves: 4
Heat Scale: Mild

JAY'S JAMAICAN JERK CHICKEN
Jay's Café at Clinton Hall, Ithaca, New York

Owner and chef Jay Solomon says that although Ithaca is far away from the sun-drenched beaches of the Caribbean, Ithacans appreciate creative cuisine and his culinary attempts to get their minds off the long winters. When he began serving this chicken dish at his restaurant, it quickly became the rage of his customers. He notes: "Jerk cooking is the Jamaican method of marinating, seasoning, and barbecuing chicken, pork, or beef. The marinade is sweet, hot, spicy, and full of complex flavors."

2   **Scotch bonnet (Habanero) chiles,** stems removed, seeded, and minced (or substitute 4 jalapeños)

6   scallions, diced

1   onion, diced

¾   cup soy sauce

½   cup red wine vinegar

¼   cup vegetable oil

¼   cup brown sugar

2   Tablespoons fresh thyme

1   teaspoon crushed whole cloves

1   teaspoon black peppercorns, crushed

½   teaspoon ground cloves

½   teaspoon ground nutmeg

½   teaspoon ground allspice

¼   teaspoon ground cinnamon

1-½   pounds chicken breasts, boned, skinned, and cut into strips

Combine all the ingredients except the chicken in a food processor and process for 10 to 15 seconds at high speed. Pour the marinade into a bowl and add the chicken. Refrigerate and marinate for 4 to 6 hours.

Remove the chicken from the marinade and drain off any excess liquid. Place on an oiled grill and cook for 4 to 5 minutes on each side, or until the chicken is cooked in the center. Serve the chicken over rice with fried plantains and okra on the side.

Serves: 4
Heat Scale: Hot

JAMAICAN-STYLE FRIED CHICKEN

Panama Red's Beach Bar and Seafood Grille, Nashville, Tennessee

Here is another variation on the use of Scotch bonnets with chicken, this one developed by owner and chef John Cowan, who says: "I am a big fan of Scotch bonnets—they are fiery, but if used correctly (and mainly in small quantities) they can add terrific flavor without overpowering a dish."

1 chicken, 3-½ pounds, quartered

4 **large Scotch bonnet (Habanero) chiles,** stems removed, seeded, and cut into thin strips

1 egg

½ cup milk

½ cup flour

1 **teaspoon red chile powder**

1 teaspoon salt

1 teaspoon black pepper

1 teaspoon white pepper

oil for frying

Make approximately 6 incisions ¾-inch deep in the flesh of each chicken quarter. Insert a slice of Scotch bonnet into each incision and let the chicken sit in the refrigerator for 24 to 48 hours, depending on how brave you are.

Mix together the egg and the milk in a mixing bowl. On a plate, mix together the dry ingredients. Dip the chicken pieces into the milk and egg, then roll them in the flour mixture. Place in a deep fryer or in a skillet filled with ¾-inch of oil. Cook at 350 degrees for 14 to 18 minutes until done.

Serve with Jamaican rice and peas and dine in a well-lit room so you can pick out the pepper slices as you eat!

Serves: 4

Heat Scale: Hot

POLLO EN MOLE ALMENDRADO
Fonda San Miguel, Austin, Texas

This chicken in almond *mole* sauce is a favorite at the Fonda San Miguel, one of the finest *haute* Mexican restaurants in the country. Chef Miguel Ravago was the first chef in Texas to introduce the complicated and diverse cuisines of Mexico, especially those of Oaxaca, Vera Cruz, Puebla, and the Yucatan.

THE CHICKEN

10 cups water
2 medium white onions, peeled and quartered
10 cloves garlic
1 cinnamon stick, 4 inches long
8 whole cloves
   salt to taste
2 chickens, cut into pieces

Bring the water to a boil and add all the ingredients. Reduce heat and simmer 25 minutes until the chicken is partially cooked. Allow it to cool in the broth, then remove from the broth and separate the meat from the bones. Reserve the meat, strain the broth, and reserve it.

MOLE ALMENDRADO

¾ cup vegetable oil
1-½ medium white onions, peeled and quartered
8 cloves garlic, peeled
2 cups blanched almonds
1 cup roasted, unsalted peanuts
1 cinnamon stick, 4 inches long
4 whole cloves
16 black peppercorns
1 croissant, torn into pieces
4 large, ripe tomatoes, roasted over open flame
4 ancho chiles, stems removed, seeded
½ cup vegetable oil
2 slices white onion
   toasted blanched almonds and sprigs of Italian parsley for garnish

Heat the oil in a large saucepan. Add the onions, garlic, almonds, peanuts, cinnamon, cloves, peppercorns, and croissant, and cook over medium heat for 25 minutes, adding more oil if the mixture begins to stick.

Remove the mixture from the heat and place it in a blender. Add the tomatoes and chiles and puree.

Heat ½ cup oil in a saucepan and brown the onion slices. Stir in the pureed mixture and cook until it releases its fat. Add the reserved chicken broth as needed to thin the sauce slightly. Add the chicken and cook an additional 25 minutes.

To serve, place the chicken in *mole* on a large clay dish and garnish with the almonds and parsley.

Serves: 8
Heat Scale: Mild

GRILLED LEMON CHICKEN
WITH MINCED CHILES
East Wind Restaurant, Alexandria, Virginia

Although not as prevalent in this country as Thai food, Vietnamese cooking is beginning to gain ground. The combination of fish sauce and hot chiles is very common in that country, and according to East Wind owner Khai Nguyen, in Vietnam "food is served with hot chiles in every meal."

½ teaspoon lemon juice
½ teaspoon ground lemon peel
1 clove garlic, minced
½ teaspoon ground peanuts
½ teaspoon ground sesame seeds
½ teaspoon soy sauce
½ **teaspoon fish sauce**
1 teaspoon sugar

¼ teaspoon black pepper
¼ teaspoon paprika
1 teaspoon honey
1 pound boned chicken breast, each breast cut into five pieces
¼ **cup serrano chiles,** stems removed, seeded and minced very fine

Combine all ingredients except the serranos and chicken and toss the chicken pieces in the marinade. Marinate the chicken for at least 2 hours. Grill the chicken over an aromatic wood such as pecan or hickory until the pieces are golden brown. Sprinkle with the serranos and serve.

Serves: 2 or 3
Heat Scale: Medium to Hot

Amazing Accompaniments

Yes, it's true, many of these hot and spicy side dishes can be—and have been—served as entrees, especially the casseroles and the stuffed chiles. But for the most part, these dishes are served to accompany the main course. They add color, flavor, nutrition, and spice to the meal. In the case where they are served with roasted or grilled meats or poultry, they may be the only spicy heat in the meal.

Quite a variety of ingredients are used in these side dishes. There are the staples: beans, corn, rice, potatoes; fresh vegetables: onions, eggplants, spinach, artichokes; and, reliably, the chiles: jalapeños, poblanos, New Mexicans, Habaneros, and more.

Here we start with a couple of interesting breads and then wander off into a world of varied culinary wonders.

ANDOUILLE AND CHILE CHEESE MUFFINS
Café Creole, Jackson, Mississippi

This Creole restaurant was opened in 1986 by owners Larry McCandless and Wayne Craft. The spicy recipes are designed by the cooking staff, which is led by Dann Plaster. These unique muffins depend on jalapeños and andouille sausage for their heat.

½ **pound minced andouille sausage**	¾ Tablespoon sage
1 Tablespoon butter	1 teaspoon poultry seasoning
½ small onion, chopped	¾ teaspoon salt
⅛ cup chopped parsley	½ teaspoon thyme
1-½ cups corn muffin mix	½ teaspoon oregano
1 egg	½ teaspoon black pepper
⅓ cup milk	½ teaspoon rosemary
⅓ bunch scallions, chopped	½ cup grated cheddar cheese
¼ **cup minced, pickled jalapeños**	

Sauté the sausage until almost brown. Drain and reserve. Sauté the onions and parsley in the butter until the onions are soft and transfer the mixture to a mixing bowl. Mix together the remaining ingredients except the sausage and cheese. When thoroughly mixed, add the sausage, whip until fully blended, and fold in the cheese. Pour the mixture into greased muffin pans and bake at 350 degrees for 12 to 15 minutes.

Yield: 10 to 12 muffins
Heat Scale: Medium to Hot

TOASTED BAGUETTES WITH CHIPOTLE CHILE BUTTER
8700 at the Citadel, Scottsdale, Arizona

Chef John Bartilomo of the 8700 Restaurant uses this smoky butter as a topping for hamburgers and steaks, as well as a spread for breads. It is in perfect harmony with his approach to food, in which he undertakes to create "something unusual and unforgettable and at the same time keep it simple."

1 pound sweet butter
1 **chipotle chile** which has been soaked in water to soften it (or more for heat)
2 Tablespoons minced chives
3 Tablespoons chopped cilantro
2 scallions, chopped
juice of 1 lime
toasted baguette slices

Cut the butter into eighths to soften and place it with the other ingredients (except the bread) in a food processor. Blend until smooth. Spread over as many baguette slices as needed.

Yield: 1 pound
Heat Scale: Mild to Medium

~~~~~~~~~~~~~~~~~~~~~

EGGPLANT EL PASO
Maria's of Keno, Klamath Falls, Oregon

This restaurant began as a catering operation and then expanded to a full-service operation seating forty-four chile addicts. Bud Spillar does the cooking and admits (tongue in cheek) that his wife Ruth helps "some." Bud says his business has "maxed out," but he refuses to expand because he doesn't want to lose personal contact with his customers. This eggplant recipe is one of his creations that utilizes traditional ingredients in an innovative manner.

OREGANO-CHILE SAUCE

½ **cup canned New Mexican green chiles,** chopped
2 quarts chicken broth
6 bay leaves
2 Tablespoons Mexican oregano
½ cup diced onions

½ cup diced fresh tomato
salt to taste
2 Tablespoons masa harina
2 Tablespoons flour
2 cups water

Combine the first 7 ingredients, bring to a boil, reduce heat, and simmer for 15 minutes. Mix the masa and flour with the water, add to the sauce, and simmer and stir constantly until reduced and thickened to the consistency of cream gravy.

Yield: 1-½ quarts

THE CASSEROLE

1 dozen eggs
2 Tablespoons garlic, minced
1 Tablespoon ground cumin
1 teaspoon salt
1 teaspoon black pepper
4 large eggplants (not peeled), sliced into ¼-inch thick slices
cracker crumbs

peanut oil for frying
Oregano-Chile Sauce
3-½ **cups canned chopped New Mexican green chiles**
¾ pound grated cheddar cheese
¾ pound grated Monterey Jack cheese

Beat the eggs with a wire whisk and add the garlic, cumin, salt, and pepper. Dip the eggplant slices into this mixture, coat with the cracker crumbs, and fry in the peanut oil at 350 degrees until golden brown. Remove and drain on paper towels.

Pour a small amount of the sauce in the bottom of a casserole dish about 8 by 13 inches and 3 inches deep. Add eggplant slices, sauce, green chiles, and cheeses. Repeat this process until there are 4 layers, the last topped with cheese. Bake in a 350 degree oven for 45 minutes.

Serves: 8 to 10
Heat Scale: Medium

NEW IBERIA RICE

K-Paul's Louisiana Kitchen,
New Orleans, Louisiana

Chef Paul Prudhomme comments: "This dish is yummy and has a moderately hot zing. Add more Meat Magic if you want more heat. It's delicious served with fresh sliced tomatoes and steamed green vegetables, and it's great stuffed in bell peppers."

3	**Tablespoons plus 2 teaspoons Meat Magic or other Cajun spice mix**	1	cup finely chopped red bell peppers
1	teaspoon dry mustard	5	cups beef stock, chilled and then skimmed of all fat
1	teaspoon dried oregano leaves	**1**	**cup finely chopped, canned New Mexican green chiles**
1	pound ground round steak	¾	cup chopped tomatoes
1-¼	cups finely chopped onions	½	teaspoon minced garlic
1-¼	cups finely chopped green or yellow bell peppers	2	cups uncooked rice (preferably converted)

Thoroughly combine the Meat Magic with the mustard and oregano in a small bowl, breaking up any lumps.

In a 4-quart saucepan (preferably not a nonstick type), combine the meat and ½ cup each of the onions, green or yellow bell peppers, and red bell peppers, breaking up the meat. Turn the heat to high, cover the pan, and cook 3 minutes. Stir well, re-cover the pan and cook 4 minutes. Stir again, breaking up any remaining chunks of meat, and add the Meat Magic mixture. Stir well, then cook uncovered for 2 minutes, stirring frequently and scraping the pan bottom well. Add 1 cup of the stock, stirring and scraping until any sediment is dissolved from the pan bottom. Cook until the mixture is fairly dry, about 6 minutes, stirring and scraping occasionally. Add ½ cup of the green chiles, the tomatoes, and the garlic. Stir well and cook 6 minutes, stirring and scraping almost constantly. Stir in the rice and the remaining ¾ cup onions, ¾ cup green or yellow bell peppers, ½ cup red bell peppers, and ½ cup chiles.

Cook, stirring constantly, until the mixture is sticking excessively, about 2 minutes. Add the remaining 4 cups stock, stirring well to dissolve any sediment from the pan bottom. Cover pan and bring to a boil, then stir and scrape well. Reduce heat to maintain a light simmer, cover the pan and cook 5 minutes, stirring and scraping frequently so mixture won't scorch. Stir again, reduce heat to very low, cover pan and cook about 25 minutes more. Remove from the heat and serve immediately.

Serves: 6 to 8
Heat Scale: Medium

~~~~~~~~~~~~~~~~~~~

SPICY BARBECUED BLACK BEANS
Routh Street Café, Dallas, Texas

A recent *Zagat Restaurant Guide* for Dallas awarded an astonishing twenty-eight points to the Routh Street Café, the highest rating for food in the Metroplex. That's not bad for chile peppers in general and chef Stephan Pyles in particular, who got his culinary start as a helper in his family's truck stop café in West Texas. Stephan and partner John Dayton also own Goodfellow's and Tejas restaurants in Minneapolis.

1 **small ancho chile,** stem removed, halved and seeded

1 **serrano chile,** stem removed, halved and seeded

1 **dried chipotle chile,** stem removed, reconstituted in water, halved and seeded

1 small ripe tomato, quartered

1 small onion, quartered

1 stalk celery

½ red bell pepper, halved and seeded

½ yellow bell pepper, halved and seeded

2 cloves garlic, peeled

1 small turnip, peeled and quartered

1 quart rich veal stock (or substitute beef stock)

2 teaspoons dry mustard

6 Tablespoons raspberry vinegar

6 Tablespoons light brown sugar

½ cup catsup

6 cups cooked black beans

Build a fire in the smoker using natural chunk charcoal. Soak aromatic wood chunks (such as hickory or pecan) in water. When the fire has burned down to coals, about 30 minutes, place the soaked wood on the coals.

Place the chiles and vegetables on the grill over indirect heat (over a pan of water if you don't have a two-part smoker) and smoke them for 20 minutes. The smoker should register 180 degrees.

Remove the chiles and vegetables from the smoker and place them in a 2-quart saucepan with the stock. Bring to a boil and reduce the liquid by one-third. Whisk in the mustard. Strain and set aside the liquid.

In a small saucepan, whisk together the vinegar and sugar. Bring to a boil and continue cooking until the mixture becomes syrupy, about 3 minutes.

Add the syrup to the strained veal stock and whisk in the catsup. Strain the sauce through a fine strainer.

Add the black beans to the stock and heat thoroughly, stirring well.

Serves: 6
Heat Scale: Medium

RED RANCH TORTELLINI
Pasqual's Southwestern Deli,
Minneapolis, Minnesota

This recipe was designed by Tim Healy, chef at the Minneapolis location of this Madison, Wisconsin–based restaurant. As an avid fan of hot and spicy foods, he was delighted when his tortellini recipe won "Best Deli Salad" in the 1990 Best of the Twin Cities Awards sponsored by the *Mpls. St. Paul Magazine*. It can be served hot as an accompaniment or cold as a salad.

1	pound tortellini, meat- or cheese-filled	1	Tablespoon cumin
	olive oil		salt and black pepper to taste
1	large onion, sliced	¼	cup olive oil
4	cloves chopped garlic	**1**	**Tablespoon adobo sauce from chipotles in adobo sauce**
3	**poblano chiles,** roasted, peeled, seeded, stems removed, cut into strips		chopped green onions for garnish
½	**cup New Mexican red chile powder**		

Boil the tortellini until done *al dente,* toss with olive oil, and set aside.

Sauté the onion, garlic, poblanos, chile powder, and spices in the ¼ cup olive oil until tender. Add the adobo sauce and mix well.

Toss this sauce with the tortellini, taking care not to break up the tortellinis. Adjust seasonings and add the green onions for garnish.

Serves: 4
Heat Scale: Hot

〰〰〰〰〰〰

GRILLED VIDALIA SWEET ONIONS WITH POBLANO CREAM
McKinnon's Louisiane Restaurant, Atlanta, Georgia

Vidalia onions, which hail from Vidalia, Georgia, are large and exceedingly sweet and juicy. They are available in May and June by mail order as well as in many supermarkets, but if you can't find them, substitute Texas sweets or Walla Wallas.

POBLANO CREAM

2 **poblano chiles,** stems removed, roasted, peeled, and seeded

½ teaspoon salt

1 bunch cilantro, leaves only

1 cup sour cream

juice of 1 lime

Combine all ingredients in a food processor and puree. Chill in the refrigerator.

Yield: 2 cups

GRILLED VIDALIA SWEET ONIONS

4 Vidalia onions, peeled, and halved along the equator

olive oil

salt and pepper

Make ¼-inch X-shaped incisions on the flat side of the onion halves without touching the 2 outside sections.

Grill the onion halves over a hot fire and partially caramelize them. Puddle some Poblano Cream on small plates and serve the onion halves in it, flat side up. Drizzle olive oil and sprinkle salt and pepper over the X-shaped incisions.

Serves: 8

Heat Scale: Mild

TILA'S REFRIED BLACK BEANS
Tila's, Chevy Chase, Maryland

This Washington, D.C.–area restaurant specializes in what it calls "creative Latino Southwest cuisine." Chef Clive DuVal III developed the concept by combining elements of the cooking of Central America (where he lived for a while, farming black beans) with that of the American

Southwest and the Orient. He likes to take traditional dishes and give them an innovative twist, as here he substitutes black beans for pinto beans for *refritos* and, instead of *queso blanco,* garnishes them with feta cheese.

1 pound dried black beans, cleaned	½ pound bacon, minced
2 small white onions, one quartered and one diced	**3 jalapeños,** stems removed, seeded, and chopped
2 cloves garlic	3 Tablespoons safflower oil
2 cups chicken stock	salt and pepper to taste
	¾ pound grated feta cheese

Place the beans in a stockpot and add water until the beans are covered by 3 inches. Cover the pot and bring to a boil, skimming off any foam. Reduce the heat to a simmer and cook for about 1 hour.

Add the quartered onion, the garlic, and the chicken stock. Simmer for another hour, skimming off the foam, until the beans are very tender and are splitting apart at the seams. Drain the beans, reserve the liquid, and let the beans cool to room temperature.

Sauté the bacon until crisp and almost burned. Pour off the fat, reserving about 3 or 4 tablespoons, and drain the bacon and reserve it. Sauté the diced onion and the jalapeños in the bacon fat until the onions are soft.

Place the beans in a blender along with 3 to 4 cups of the reserved liquid. Add the bacon, onion, and jalapeños, and any remaining bacon fat. Puree to a thick but still chunky consistency. Depending on the size of the blender, this process may have to be done in several batches.

Oil a sauté pan with the safflower oil and cook the beans, stirring constantly, until most of the liquid is evaporated, about 5 to 10 minutes. Remember that cooked black beans burn easily, so don't rush this process.

Serve with feta cheese sprinkled on top.

Serves: 6
Heat Scale: Medium

ORZO FROM HELL
Too Chez, Novi, Michigan

The executive chef at Too Chez, Edward Janos, says that chile peppers and sauces make ordinary foods exciting. Sometimes, as in this orzo recipe, chiles make them dynamite. Orzo is a rice-shaped pasta slightly smaller than a pine nut, often used as a substitute for rice. This dish, which is a signature menu item, is so hot and is served in such quantities that the restaurant advertises that if guests can eat it all, it's free.

½ cup olive oil
1 Habanero chile, stem removed, minced with seeds
1 serrano chile, stem removed, minced with seeds
1 large poblano chile, stem removed and julienned
2 cloves garlic, minced
10 medium shiitake mushrooms, julienned
¾ cup scallions, minced
8 cups orzo pasta, cooked *al dente*

2 cups spinach, roughly chopped
1-½ cup broccoli, blanched and chopped
6 Tablespoons fresh basil, chopped fine
salt to taste
1 Tablespoon Habanero hot sauce, such as Melinda's
1 cup reduced chicken stock
1 cup grated Parmesan-Reggiano cheese

Heat the olive oil and quickly sauté the Habanero, serrano, poblano, garlic, mushrooms, and scallions together for about 2 minutes, stirring constantly.

Add the orzo, spinach, broccoli, and basil, and cook until heated through, stirring. Add the salt, hot sauce, and chicken stock, and cook until heated through, stirring constantly.

Serve the pasta topped with the cheese.

Serves: 8
Heat Scale: Hot

POTATO-STUFFED CHILES
8700 at the Citadel, Scottsdale, Arizona

At the 8700, chef John Bartilomo specializes in Southwestern cuisine and has an interesting theory about the use of chiles. He says the appropriate amount of heat depends on your mood and attitude when you dine. If you are interested in wine and fine dining, "some spice is nice but nothing too hot." On the other hand, "if your mood is casual, I add more spice." Below is his innovative side dish combining chiles and potatoes—undoubtedly for fine dining.

1   egg yolk
1   Tablespoon sour cream
½ **teaspoon crushed New Mexican red chile**
1   large potato, baked
    salt to taste

1 **large green New Mexican chile,** split lengthwise, stem and seeds removed
minced fresh chives for garnish

Whisk together the egg yolk, sour cream, and red chile. Scoop the potato out of its skin, add to the mixture, and whisk until smooth. Add salt to taste. Fill a pastry bag with this mixture and, using a star tip, pipe it into each chile pepper half.

    Bake the chiles in a 400 degree oven until golden brown, about 15 minutes. Sprinkle with the chives and serve.

Serves: 2
Heat Scale: Mild

~~~~~~~~~~~~~~~~~~~~

LEONARDO'S MEXICAN PINTO BEANS
Leonardo's, Houston, Texas

Leonard Johnson, owner and chef of Leonardo's, grew up along the Gulf Coast of Texas and says that's why he prefers a "minimalist peasant preparation concentrating on locally grown herbs and spices." Regarding this recipe, he notes: "I prefer to drink the broth straight—you can have the beans."

6 **New Mexican green chiles,** stems removed, roasted, peeled, seeded, and chopped fine

4 **jalapeños, whole**

2 quarts chicken stock, skimmed

3 to 4 bunches green onions, chopped fine

1 pound dried pinto beans

1 whole ham bone and rind

3 cloves garlic
   pinch of cumin

Place all ingredients in a stock pot and bring to a hard boil. Boil for five minutes, then reduce heat and simmer until the beans are tender, 4 to 5 hours.

Serves: 6 to 8
Heat Scale: Medium

wwwwwwwww

ARTICHOKE HEART AND GREEN CHILE RAMEKINS
The Santa Fe Café, Seattle, Washington

Greg Gibbons, chef at the Santa Fe Café, believes in cooking that emphasizes genuine flavors and few adornments. He shies away from complicated garnishes and prefers to show the natural colors and beauty of the food. These ramekins, which are small and individually baked, are served with baguette slices as a tasty side dish or appetizer.

½	**cup chopped hot green New Mexican chiles,** roasted, peeled, seeds and stems removed	1-½	cups kasseri cheese
		1	cup mayonnaise
		2	Tablespoons minced garlic
¼	**teaspoon dried red chile flakes**		garlic butter
		4	baguette slices
1-½	cups coarsely chopped artichoke hearts in water		red chile powder for garnish
			quartered artichoke hearts for garnish
½	red bell pepper, cored and chopped		

Preheat the oven to 350 degrees. Combine the first seven ingredients in a bowl and mix well. Divide the mixture among 4 5-ounce ramekins. Bake until golden brown, about 25 minutes.

Preheat the broiler. Spread garlic butter over the baguette slices and broil until golden brown. Sprinkle lightly with chile powder.

Garnish the ramekins with quartered artichoke hearts and serve immediately with the baguette slices.

Serves: 4
Heat Scale: Medium

∿∿∿∿∿∿∿∿∿

CHILES RELLENOS
WITH SMOKED CHICKEN
Campton Place Hotel, San Francisco, California

From New Orleans to New York City to Denver to San Francisco, executive chef Jan Birnbaum has been exploring the variations of American cuisine. At the Campton Place, one of San Francisco's more elegant restaurants, he experiments with a range of Southwestern classics, as in this version of stuffed chiles.

SPINACH-TOMATILLO SAUCE

2 **poblano chiles,** stems removed, roasted, peeled, and seeded
16 tomatillos
¼ bunch fresh cilantro
4 Tablespoons lime juice
20 spinach leaves
salt and pepper to taste

Place all ingredients in a blender and blend until smooth. Warm the sauce over low heat.

Yield: 1 cup
Heat scale: Mild

THE BATTER

1-¼ cups all-purpose flour
pinch baking powder
½ teaspoon salt
2 egg yolks
1 bottle of beer
2 egg whites

Mix together the dry ingredients. Combine the beer and the egg yolks and mix gently with the flour. Whip the whites to a medium peak and fold into the flour mixture. Let sit 1 hour.

THE CHILES

15 **green New Mexican chiles,** roasted, peeled, stems on
1 whole egg
1 egg yolk
12 ounces ricotta cheese
10 ounces goat cheese
4 ounces grated mozzarella or jack cheese
4 ounces grated Parmesan or asiago cheese
bottled hot sauce to taste
½ cup chopped cilantro
3 cups smoked chicken
salt and pepper to taste
the batter
vegetable oil for deep frying
Spinach-Tomatillo Sauce
cilantro sprigs for garnish

Cut a slit in the chiles near the stem and remove the seeds. Whisk the egg and the yolk until foamy. Add the ricotta and mix thoroughly. With a rubber spatula, fold in the goat cheese. Add the remaining cheeses, hot sauce, cilantro, chicken, salt, and pepper and fold together, mixing thoroughly. Chill until very cold.

Stuff the chiles with the filling, coat them with the batter, and deep fry at 350 degrees for 4 to 6 minutes.

Spoon some warm sauce out on plates, and place the chiles on top. Garnish with sprigs of cilantro.

Yield: 15 chiles
Heat Scale: Medium

wwwwwwwwww

CHILES EN NOGADA
Zarela Restaurant, New York, New York

Here is another variation on stuffed chiles, this one courtesy of Zarela Martinez, who says that her version is based on the classic recipe served on national holidays in Mexico. She, however, bakes the chiles instead of deep frying them and eliminates the walnuts that give the dish its name. No matter—Zarela says the dish is "one of our most beloved at Zarela."

SALSA DE TOMATE ASADO

1-½ cups heavy cream
6   medium garlic cloves, unpeeled
1   medium onion, unpeeled, halved crosswise

3 to 4 large tomatoes (2-¾ pounds)
salt to taste

In a small saucepan, simmer the cream until reduced to about 1 cup.

In a large skillet or griddle, roast the garlic cloves and the onion over high heat, turning several times, until the garlic is dark on all sides and somewhat softened, and the onion is partly charred. Add the tomatoes and roast until the skins start coming off.

Peel the garlic, onions, and tomatoes and add to a blender. It's okay if a few charred bits get into the mixture. Puree on medium speed until smooth. Add the cream and repeat. Season with salt to taste and keep warm.

Yield: 2 to 3 cups

THE STUFFED POBLANOS

1	stick unsalted butter	1-½	teaspoons ground cinnamon, Ceylon preferred
1	medium onion, chopped		
2	medium garlic cloves, minced	¼	teaspoon ground cloves
½	cup pimiento-stuffed green olives, sliced	2	cups shredded cooked chicken
½	cup each pitted prunes, dried apricots, and dried peaches, diced		salt to taste
		6	**large green poblano chiles,** roasted, peeled, seeded, stems left on
1-½	teaspoons cumin seed, ground		Salsa de Tomate Asado

Melt the butter in a saucepan and sauté the onion and garlic until the onion is soft. Add the olives and the fruits and continue to sauté until the fruits are soft. Add the spices and cook 1 more minute. Combine this mixture with the shredded chicken and mix well. Adjust for salt.

Carefully fill the chiles with the mixture and bake on a greased baking sheet for 7 minutes at 350 degrees.

To serve, spoon the salsa on individual plates and place one chile on each plate over the salsa.

Serves: 6
Heat Scale: Mild

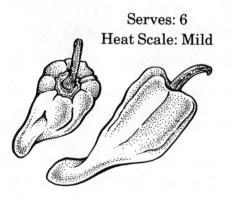

OUTLAWS CAMPFIRE PINTOS
Outlaws Steakhouse and Cantina, Orlando, Florida

On the menu at Outlaws, some selections are indicated with a howling coyote, which, according to owner Bill Hattaway, means that the dish is "mouth-scorchin', tongue-burnin', lip-peeling HOT." Sometimes, as with this recipe, Bill says: "Maybe we exaggerate justa tad."

6   **ounces chorizo sausage**
1   cup sliced green onions with tops
1   **cup canned, diced New Mexican green chile**
6   cups canned pinto beans
1   cup chopped tomato
¼   teaspoon salt
1   Tablespoon minced cilantro
1   Tablespoon crushed garlic

Sauté the onions with the sausage until brown and drain off excess fat. Combine this mixture with the remaining ingredients in an ungreased 2-quart casserole dish and bake uncovered at 350 degrees for 30 minutes.

Serves: 8
Heat Scale: Medium

SPICY VIDALIA ONION AND RED SKIN POTATO SALAD
The Original Alan's Cubana, Gainesville, Florida

This restaurant keeps over sixty hot sauces on hand for their customers to sample and, in addition, also produces a barbecue sauce with locally produced chiles. "I try to incorporate a little heat into many dishes in the form of fresh chiles, which I grow," says owner and cook Chuck Kinard. (He denies he is a chef.) "We go overboard and serve hot sauces with popcorn because it's a great way to try a new hot sauce—especially with a cold beer." The Cubana has seventeen beers on tap and a hundred more varieties in bottles. This recipe for spicy potato salad is great for serving at a large party or picnic.

4   pounds new or red skin
     potatoes
½   teaspoon each for boiling: salt,
     black pepper, **cayenne
     powder,** garlic, and onion
     powder
3   Vidalia or other sweet onions,
     diced
2   Tablespoons olive oil
3   stalks celery, diced
4   cloves garlic, minced
½   teaspoon garlic powder
½   teaspoon olive oil
1   teaspoon celery root powder
     (available in health food
     stores), or substitute celery
     salt
2   Tablespoons apple cider
     vinegar
½   teaspoon salt
½   **teaspoon cayenne powder**
¼   teaspoon white pepper
¼   teaspoon freshly ground black
     pepper
½   teaspoon tarragon leaves
¼   teaspoon dried thyme
¼   teaspoon Hungarian paprika
½   teaspoon dry mustard
½   teaspoon garlic powder
1   cup mayonnaise
½   cup sour cream
¼   **cup jalapeño chiles,** stems
     removed, seeded, and
     minced

Place the potatoes with skins on in a pan and cover with enough water by 2 to 3 inches. Add ½ teaspoon of salt, black pepper, cayenne, garlic, and onion powder and boil until done but somewhat firm. Cool the potatoes and then dice them with the skins and place in a large bowl.

Sauté ⅔ of the onions in 2 tablespoons olive oil until they start to turn brown. Add them to the potatoes along with the remaining ingredients (including the remaining raw onion) except the jalapeños, and mix well. Chill the potato salad and sprinkle with the minced jalapeños before serving.

Serves: 8 to 10
Heat Scale: Hot

Calming Cool-Downs and Devilish Desserts

Although chile peppers occasionally appear in drinks like Bloody Marys and desserts like our final two recipes, for the most part the recipes in this chapter are used to cool down over-stimulated taste buds and to refresh the palate.

Many cultures have their own cool-downs. The Chinese use white rice, the Vietnamese suggest hot liquids such as tea, and the Mexicans insist that if enough beer is consumed, no one will care how hot the chiles are! Other suggested cool-down cures include water, syrups, and other sugar-based concoctions. None of these are very effective in actually countering capsaicin (the pungent compound in chiles), but they do provide a cool sensation on a burned palate.

The only cool-downs that can provide immediate relief from the burning sensation of capsaicin are dairy products such as milk, cream, sour cream, yogurt, and ice cream. For some reason, cheese does not seem to have the same effect. Milk can be consumed with the meal to cut the heat, and sour cream or yogurt can be served on the side for the same purpose.

As we see from these recipes, dairy products can easily be incorporated into both drinks and desserts to provide cooling relief. Some chileheads swear that fruits also cut heat, so some fruit drinks and desserts are also included in this chapter.

And not to let you off easy, the last two recipes prove that desserts, too, can be devilish.

THREE TROPICAL COOLERS
The Original Alan's Cubana, Gainesville, Florida

This restaurant, across from the University of Florida, is decorated in "rustic nautical" decor along with some beer-related items because of their collection of beers from all over the world. In addition to providing brews to cool down his spicy food, owner Chuck Kinard serves up some refreshing fruit drinks, like these three variations on a theme.

TROPICAL COOLER #1

¼ cup frozen raspberries
¼ cup crushed pineapple
½ cup white seedless grapes
¾ cup ripe cantaloupe or honeydew melon
1-½ cups frozen vanilla yogurt

Place all ingredients in a blender or food processor and mix until smooth. Chill and serve.

Yield: 3 cups
Sweet Scale: Medium

TROPICAL COOLER #2

1 cup fresh mango
¼ cup fresh kiwi fruit
¼ cup freshly squeezed orange juice
1 teaspoon cream of coconut
½ cup frozen vanilla yogurt

Place all ingredients in a blender or food processor and mix until smooth. Chill and serve.

Yield: 2 cups
Sweet Scale: Medium

TROPICAL COOLER #3

1 cup fresh nectarine
¼ cup crushed pineapple
½ cup whole milk
½ cup freshly squeezed orange juice
½ cup pineapple juice
2 cups frozen vanilla yogurt

Place all ingredients in a blender or food processor and mix until smooth. Chill and serve.

Yield: 4-½ cups
Sweet Scale: Medium

AGUA FRESCA DE TAMARINDO
Pinch-a-Pollo Restaurant, Austin, Texas

Robb Walsh, a friend and fellow food writer who lives in Austin, collected this recipe during a hot and spicy reconnaissance visit to this restaurant, which features sixteen different hot sauces. He wrote: "On a really hot summer day in the Southwest, this is the perfect drink. I like beer too, but you can only drink so many of them. *Agua Fresca* is thirst-quenching, has more nutritive value than tea or water, and you can drink lots without worrying about caffeine or alcohol. Kids love it, and it goes great with spicy food too!"

½ pound tamarind beans	1 gallon water
¾ cup of sugar or honey	

Rinse the beans and drain them. Put the beans in a soup pot and add enough water to cover them. Cook at a low boil for ten minutes or so. Mash the softened beans vigorously with a potato masher. Strain the coffee-colored liquid into a gallon container, throwing away the seeds and outer pods as you go. Add the sugar or honey while the liquid is hot. Add water to fill the container. Refrigerate and serve over ice.

Yield: 1 gallon
Sweet Scale: Medium

Variations: Adjust the sugar level to your taste. Use the specified equivalent amount of artificial sweetener for the diet version. Serve over more or less ice to make it as strong or weak as you like it.

〰〰〰〰〰〰〰

SLOW TRAIN TO MAZATLAN
Brick Alley Pub and Restaurant, Newport, Rhode Island

Chef Ralph Plumb admits that he blatantly borrowed this recipe from "the most notorious cantina in all of Mexico, Tommy D's in Mazatlan." It is traditionally served in a pint mason jar.

½ banana
5 strawberries
½ ounce peach brandy
¾ ounce light rum

¾ ounce dark rum
1 ounce lemon sweet-and-sour
    mix

Place all ingredients in a blender with crushed ice and blend.

Serves: 1
Sweet Scale: Low

〰〰〰〰〰〰〰

NEW MEXICO FLAN
El Patio, Albuquerque, New Mexico

Since El Patio serves perhaps the hottest chile of any restaurant in New Mexico, it is only fitting that chef Tom Baca would have a traditional custard dessert to cool down overheated palates.

1-½	cups sugar	1	teaspoon vanilla extract
3	eggs	12	ounces evaporated milk
1	teaspoon almond extract		

Blend 1 cup of the sugar with the eggs and extracts until smooth. Add the milk and stir slowly until smooth, taking care not to let the mixture become foamy.

Heat remaining ½ cup of sugar until it caramelizes and turns slightly brown. Pour the caramelized sugar into a 9-inch pie pan and then pour the egg mixture over the top.

Place the pie pan in a large pan with ¼ inch of water in it and bake in a 350 degree oven for 45 minutes to an hour. Remove from the oven and chill before serving. To serve, scoop out a portion of flan, flip it over on a dessert plate, and spoon extra syrup from the bottom of the pie pan over it.

Serves: 4 to 6
Sweet Scale: Medium

〜〜〜〜〜〜〜〜〜〜

KAHLÚA MOUSSE
El Torito Restaurants, Irvine, California

First established in 1954, El Torito pioneered the format of the Mexican dinnerhouse where one could dine in a pleasant atmosphere and feast on fine Sonoran-style Mexican food. Previously, Mexican food was available in California only at stands or mom-and-pop operations. This mousse is one of the restaurant's most popular desserts.

2	cups whipped non-dairy topping	3	Tablespoons granulated sugar
½	cup heavy whipping cream	6	Tablespoons Kahlúa brand liqueur
1	Tablespoon instant coffee		
2	Tablespoons unsweetened cocoa powder		

Whip the non-dairy topping with the whipping cream until stiff. Add the coffee, cocoa, and sugar and blend. Add the Kahlúa and stir into the mixture with a rubber spatula. Chill the mousse.

When ready to serve, the mousse can be topped with whipped cream, chocolate sprinkles, and a wafer cookie.

Serves: 8
Sweet Scale: High

SOUTHWESTERN BREAD PUDDING WITH TEQUILA SAUCE
The Pink Adobe, Santa Fe, New Mexico

In 1944, World War II was still raging, your editor was born, and Rosalea Murphy opened "The Pink" in Santa Fe. The restaurant seated only thirty, and the menu was brief, but customers loved Rosalea's eclectic creations and the restaurant flourished. Nearly a half-century later, it's still one of the top five restaurants in "The City Different."

TEQUILA SAUCE

1   cup sugar
1   egg
1   stick butter, melted

⅓   cup good-quality tequila
1   teaspoon fresh lime juice

Cream the sugar and egg together. Add the butter and pour into a medium saucepan. Over low heat, stir the mixture until the sugar is dissolved. Remove from the heat and stir in the tequila and lime juice.

Yield: 1 cup
Sweet Scale: High

SOUTHWESTERN BREAD PUDDING

½   pound stale French bread
1   cup milk
1   stick butter, melted
½   cup golden raisins
¼   cup piñons
3   eggs, beaten
1-¼ cups sugar
1   4-ounce can evaporated
    milk
1   8¼-ounce can crushed
    pineapple with juice
1   Tablespoon fresh lemon
    juice
1   Tablespoon vanilla
    Tequila Sauce

Preheat the oven to 350 degrees. Break the bread into bite-sized chunks and soak them in the milk for a few minutes. Squeeze the bread to eliminate excess liquid and discard the milk. Place the bread in a large bowl and add the remaining ingredients. Mix thoroughly but gently. Pour the mixture into an 8- by 12-inch buttered baking pan and bake for 1 hour or until a knife inserted in the center comes out clean. Serve by pouring Tequila Sauce over individual portions.

Serves: 8 to 10
Sweet Scale: Medium

〰〰〰〰〰

TILA'S MANGO SORBET WITH RASPBERRY SAUCE

Tila's, Chevy Chase, Maryland

Chef Clive Duval III studied religion in England, mined silver and grew lemon grass in Central America, learned classic French cooking techniques at the Philadelphia Restaurant School, and finally, opened the first Tila's in Houston in 1981. In 1988, he opened the second Tila's to acclaim, as the restaurant was featured in *Esquire*'s "Best New Restaurants of 1988." We asked Chef Duval for a cooling dessert, and he responded with the following creation.

MANGO SORBET

2 large mangoes, peeled, pitted, and chopped

2 Tablespoons lime juice
¼ cup sugar syrup

Combine all ingredients in a food processor and puree until smooth. Freeze until solid.

RASPBERRY SAUCE

2 cups raspberries, fresh preferred

2 Tablespoons sugar (or more to taste)

juice of 1 lime

Combine all ingredients in a blender and puree until smooth. Transfer to a pan and bring to a boil, then reduce heat and simmer until thickened. Add a little arrowroot to thicken or a little rum to thin the sauce. Allow to cool and serve the sauce over the sorbet.

Serves: 4 to 6
Sweet Scale: Medium

~~~~~~~~~~~~~~

PRICKLY PEAR SABAYON IN A
SWEET CINNAMON CHALUPA SHELL

Piñon Grill, Inn at McCormick Ranch,
Scottsdale, Arizona

Chef Farn Boggie has outdone himself with this creation, which features the flavors of the Southwest combined with the techniques of France and Italy. *Chalupa* is Spanish for "boat" and describes the shell in which the filling is placed. Chalupa shell baskets for deep frying are available from mail order kitchen shops.

3 prickly pear pads *(nopales)*, peeled and diced	4 6-inch flour tortillas cinnamon sugar
½ cup sugar	
½ cup water	4 fresh raspberries for garnish whipped cream for garnish
4 eggs, separated	
½ pint warm, heavy cream	

Place the pads in a small saucepan with the sugar and water and boil until the sugar dissolves. Puree the mixture in a blender until smooth and set aside.

Add the prickly pear puree to the egg yolks in a bowl. Place the bowl in boiling water and whip the yolks until the mixture is firm and keeps its shape. Slowly add in the heavy cream, mix, and taste for sugar. Add more if necessary. Remove from heat and set aside.

Whip the egg whites into stiff peaks and then fold them into the sabayon sauce. Set aside.

Deep fry the tortillas into the shape of a basket by using a ladle to hold the tortillas under the oil. When crisp, remove from oil. Dust the shells with cinnamon and sugar.

Place the chalupa on a salad plate, fill with the prickly pear sabayon, and garnish with raspberries and whipped cream.

Serves: 4
Sweet Scale: Medium

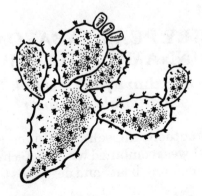

TOASTED CHILE CUSTARD
Fourth Street Grill, Berkeley, California

The Fourth Street Grill is so famous for its hot and spicy meals that for years owner Susan Nelson has served all-chile dinners during a two-week period in August. Chiles of varying heat levels appear in every course from appetizers to desserts such as this one, which was created by chef Nathan Peterson.

2   eggs
2   egg yolks
⅓   cup brown sugar, plus 2
      Tablespoons for the topping
¼   teaspoon salt

2   cups cream
¼   teaspoon vanilla
**2   teaspoons powdered chile
      de arbol,** toasted

Wisk the eggs and egg yolks with ⅓ cup brown sugar and salt until just mixed.

Scald the cream with the vanilla. Add half of the cream to the egg mixture, stirring constantly. Add the mixture to the remainder of the cream and cook over low heat, stirring constantly, until the custard coats the spoon.

Pour the custard into 4 4-ounce ramekins and place in a water bath. Bake at 300 degrees for 35 minutes until the custard sets. Cool for 3 hours in the refrigerator before serving.

To Serve: Sprinkle ¼ teaspoon chile powder over the top of each custard and then top with a thin layer of sifted brown sugar. Place the custard under the broiler, watching constantly, until the sugar is melted but not burned. Serve immediately.

Serves: 4
Heat Scale: Mild
Sweet Scale: Medium

CREPES SUZETTE DIABLE
W. C. Longacre Catering Company, Albuquerque, New Mexico

Chef Longacre has always enjoyed cooking and originally opened his first restaurant, The Morning Glory Café, in Albuquerque, so he could raise enough money to put himself through chiropractic school. "But I liked cooking so much, it became a passion with me and I could never give it up," he says. One of his trademarks is using chile peppers in nearly every dish, as he does in this variation on a classic dessert.

THE CREPES

¾	cup milk
¾	cup cold water
3	egg yolks
1	Tablespoon white granulated sugar

3	Tablespoons Grand Marnier liqueur
1-½	cups sifted all-purpose flour
5	Tablespoons melted butter

Place the ingredients in a blender in the same order they are listed and blend at top speed for one minute. Cover and refrigerate for a minium of 2 hours.

To cook the crepes, brush a 7-inch cast iron skillet with vegetable oil and place on medium heat until it begins to smoke. Remove from heat and ladle in approximately 2 ounces of batter, rolling the skillet to cover the entire bottom evenly with a thin layer. Return the skillet to the heat for 60 to 80 seconds, loosen the crepe with a spatula, turn, and cook for an additional 30 seconds. Remove and repeat the process, stacking the crepes and covering them with waxed paper.

TO ASSEMBLE AND SERVE

½ cup butter
2 Tablespoons frozen orange juice concentrate
1 Tablespoon Grand Marnier liqueur
1 jalapeño, stem removed, seeded, and minced fine
grated rind from 1 orange
The Crepes

1 Tablespoon sugar, plus additional sugar for sprinkling
2 ounces brandy
1 ounce Grand Marnier liqueur
½ **Teaspoon Louisiana-style hot sauce**

Cream the butter in a mixing bowl. Gradually beat in the orange juice, 1 tablespoon sugar, 1 tablespoon Grand Marnier, the jalapeño, and the orange rind. Beat until most of the liquid has been absorbed by the butter.

When you are ready to serve the crepes, add the orange butter to a large skillet and heat until the butter melts. Pick up one crepe and dip it in the orange butter, then quickly turn it and coat the other side. Fold it in half and then fold it again. Push it to one side of the pan and repeat the process until all the crepes have been coated and folded in a single layer in the skillet.

Sprinkle the crepes with sugar. Combine the brandy, Grand Marnier, and the hot sauce and pour the mixture over the crepes. Allow it to heat for a few seconds, carefully light the mixture with a match, and serve the flaming, spicy hot crepes.

Yield: 12 crepes
Heat Scale: Medium
Sweet Scale: Mild

APPENDIX:
PARTICIPATING
RESTAURANTS

Bayou Bar and Grill
329 Market Street
San Diego, CA 92101

Bombay Café
11213 Santa Monica Boulevard,
  #205
Los Angeles, CA 90025

Brick Alley Pub and Restaurant
140 Thames Street
Newport, RI 02840

Café Creole
5852 Ringewood Road
Jackson, MS 39158

Calypso Caribbean Cuisine
5555 Morningside Drive
Houston, TX 77005

Campton Place Hotel
340 Stockton Street
San Francisco, CA 94108

**The Cantina Tex-Mex Bar and
  Grill**
3011 Hillsborough Street
Raleigh, NC 27607

La Casa Sena
20 Sena Plaza, 125 East Palace
  Avenue
Santa Fe, NM 87501

La Cazuela
7 Old South Street
Northampton, MA 01060

El Cholo Mexican Restaurant
1121 South Western Avenue
Los Angeles, CA 90006

Claire Restaurant
156 Seventh Avenue
New York, NY 10011

**Compadres Mexican Bar and
  Grill**
1200 Ala Moana Boulevard
Honolulu, HI 96814

Coyote Café
132 West Water Street
Santa Fe, NM 87501

The Crazy Flamingo
1049 N. Collier Boulevard
Marco Island, FL 33937

Culinary Capers
5706 Woodcrest Avenue
Baltimore, MD 21215

East Coast Grill
1271 Cambridge Street
Cambridge, MA 02139

East Wind Restaurant
809 King Street
Alexandria, VA 22314

8700 at the Citadel Pinnacle Peak
8700 East Pinnacle Peak Road
Scottsdale, AZ 85255

Firehouse Bar-B-Que
1420 Burlingame Avenue
Burlingame, CA 94010

Fonda San Miguel
2330 W. North Loop Boulevard
Austin, TX 78756

Fourth Street Grill
1820 Fourth Street
Berkeley, CA 94704

Galley del Mar
880 Lake Harbor Drive
Ridgeland, MS 39157

Great Jones Café
54 Great Jones Street
New York, NY 10012

J.J. and Co. Restaurant and Bar
11 G Street
San Rafael, CA 94901

Jay's Café at Clinton Hall
114 N. Cayuga Street
Ithaca, NY 14850

Jeffrey's
1202 West Lynn
Austin, TX 78703

K-Paul's Louisiana Kitchen
415 Chartres Street
New Orleans, LA 70116

L.A. Nicola Restaurant
4326 Sunset Boulevard
Los Angeles, CA 90028

Leonardo's
5420 LBJ Freeway, Suite 200
Dallas, TX 75240

The Loon Café
500 First Avenue North
Minneapolis, MN 55403

Majestic Diner
1806 Barton Springs Road
Austin, TX 78704

The Mansion on Turtle Creek
2821 Turtle Creek Boulevard
Dallas, TX 75219

Maple Leaf Grill
8909 Roosevelt Way
Seattle, WA 98115

Maria's of Keno
2424 Shasta Way
Klamath Falls, OR 97603

McKinnon's Louisiane Restaurant
3209 Maple Drive
Atlanta, GA 30305

The Mex
185 Main Street
Ellsworth, ME 04605

Mildred's VIP Catering
1841 County Line Road
Jackson, MS 39213

Miss Pearl's Jam House
601 Eddy at Larkin
San Francisco, CA 94109

El Norteño
7306 Zuni Road S.E.
Albuquerque, NM 87108

On the Verandah
U.S. 64
Highlands, NC 28741

The Original Alan's Cubana
1712 W. University Avenue
Gainesville, FL 32604

Outlaws Steakhouse and Cantina
3552 East Colonial Drive
Orlando, FL 32803

Panama Red's
1901 Broadway
Nashville, TN 37203

Pasqual's Southwestern Deli
2534 Monroe Street
Madison, WI 53711

La Paz Restaurante
6410 Roswell Road
Atlanta, GA 30328

Pecos River Café
1501 York Avenue
New York, NY 10021

The Pickled Parrot
26 North 5th Street
Minneapolis, MN 55043

The Pier House
#1 Duvall Street
Key West, FL 33040

Pinch-a-Pollo
7915 Burnet Road
Austin, TX 78758

The Pink Adobe
406 Old Santa Fe Trail
Santa Fe, NM 87502

Piñon Grill
The Inn at McCormick Ranch
7401 North Scottsdale Road
Scottsdale, AZ 85253

Quaker Steak and Lube
110 Connelly Boulevard
Sharon, PA 16146

The Rattlesnake Club
300 River Place
Detroit, MI 48207

Restaurant André
1100 San Mateo Boulevard N.E.
Albuquerque, NM 87110

Restaurant Muse
1559-E Pacific Coast Highway, Suite 608
Hermosa Beach, CA 90254

The Riverwood
Route 3, Box 908
Boone, NC 28607

Routh Street Café
3005 Routh Street
Dallas, TX 75201

Rudy V's Restaurant
4501 Eastgate Boulevard
Cincinnati, OH 45245

Santa Fe Café
5910 Phinney Avenue North
Seattle, WA 98103

Silverheels Southwest Grill
81 Buffalo Drive, Wildernest
Silverthorne, CO 80498

Sim's Catering and Deli
65 East Washington Avenue
Washington, NJ 07882

Texas Chili and Rib Company
2948 East Bell Road
Phoenix, AZ 85259

Tila's Restaurant and Bar
2 Wisconsin Circle
Chevy Chase, MD 20815

Too Chez
27115 Sheraton Drive
Novi, MI 48337

El Torito Restaurants
Corporate Offices
2450 White Road
Irvine, CA 92713

La Tour Restaurant
Park Hyatt Hotel
800 N. Michigan Avenue
Chicago, IL 60611

**W. C. Longacre Catering
Company**
834 Gabaldon N.W.
Albuquerque, NM 87104

Zarela Restaurant
953 Second Avenue
New York, NY 10022

Zia Café
421 North Milpas
Santa Barbara, CA 93101

INDEX